MONSTER FILES

Monster Files

A Look Inside Government Secrets and Classified Documents on Bizarre Creatures and Extraordinary Animals

Nick Redfern

This edition first published in 2013 by New Page Books, an imprint of
Red Wheel/Weiser, LLC
With offices at:
65 Parker Street, Suite 7
Newburyport, MA 01950
www.redwheelweiser.com
www.newpagebooks.com

ISBN: 978-1-60163-263-0
Library of Congress Cataloging-in-Publication Data
Redfern, Nicholas, 1964-
  Monster files : a look inside government secrets and classified docu-
ments on bizarre creatures and extraordinary animals / by Nick Redfern.
    pages cm
  Includes bibliographical references and index.
  ISBN 978-1-60163-263-0 (print) -- ISBN 978-1-60163-530-3 (ebook) 1.
Monsters. 2. Animals, Mythical. I. Title.

  GR825.R434 2013
  001.944--dc23

                                    2013007276
Cover design by noir33
Interior by Gina Talucci

Printed in the United States of America
IBI
10 9 8 7 6 5 4 3 2 1

DEDICATION

For Tim Binnall who, in 2012, asked me, "Nick, why don't you write a book about Cryptozoology and the government?" Well, Tim, thanks to your brilliant suggestion, now I have!

Contents

INTRODUCTION

For decades, rumors, tales, and legends have surfaced to the effect that government agencies all around the world, since at least the 1800s, have been secretly collecting and carefully studying data on bizarre beasts, extraordinary animals, and strange creatures. Lake monsters; psychic dogs and cats; sea serpents; flying nightmares; and huge, hair-covered man-beasts—all have attracted official, classified interest. Now, for the first time, the complete, fearsome facts can finally be revealed. These facts beg some amazing and possibly paradigm-changing questions. For example: Does the Pentagon's top brass secretly have one or more dead Bigfoots on ice, deep in a secure underground bunker somewhere? If so, has a study of these unique specimens revealed the creatures to be apes of a type that zoology has yet to officially categorize? Or are they something far weirder? Might they possibly, and incredibly, be entities linked to the many and varied mysteries that accompany the UFO phenomenon? What bizarre truths are the militaries of the United States and the United Kingdom hiding from us regarding long-necked lake monsters? Are they really surviving example of prehistoric creatures that (as we are assured) became extinct millions of years ago? Or could they, in some convoluted fashion, be the curious creations of government itself?

Might there be a link between the clandestine and controversial operations of the Central Intelligence Agency (CIA) and those dark and diabolical denizens of the Himalayas known as the Abominable Snowmen? Does the CIA have secret knowledge in its possession that this immense and legendary creature—also referred to as the Yeti—really does exist? Or does officialdom's interest in the hairy beast revolve around matters that have far less to do with the world of monster hunting and far *more* to do with top-secret espionage that dates back to the height of the Cold War?

Why does an old and faded British government file exist on sightings of leviathans of the seas? Is Britain's Royal Navy sitting on amazing classified evidence suggesting that such sea-creatures really are among us and are not just the stuff of seafaring legend?

What, if anything, do the Russians know about both extrasensory perception and life after death in animals? Has the Kremlin really discovered that animals have souls and that bodily death is not the end of life as we know it? Did the United States Army use psychic dogs in covert military missions against the former Soviet Union, at the height of the Cold War?

Are presumed-extinct animals—creatures that range from gigantic marauding lizards to one of the strangest marsupials that ever existed—still roaming around the forests of Australia?

And finally, what is the top-secret connection between the late Diana, Princess of Wales, and large, savage cats prowling around the foggy and mysterious wilds of southwest England? How could there even be such a connection in the first place between the highest echelons of Britain's royal family and exotic felines that the government of the United Kingdom assures both its citizens and the media are nothing more than the results of mistaken identity and folklore combined into one controversial brew?

These are just a few of the many thought-provoking questions posed—and duly answered—in this book. In the pages that follow, you will learn the startling truths concerning how, why, when, and where agencies of government have taken an astonishing and abiding interest in those legendary creatures that mainstream science and zoology assure us do not, and simply cannot, exist. You will also learn how terrible freaks of nature were created by crazed Dr. Frankenstein–like scientists and psychological warfare experts, all operating behind a near-impenetrable cloak of official sanction and secrecy.

Monsters are not just the stuff of myth, fantasy, legend, and folklore. In their own very odd and unique ways, some of them are all too terrifyingly real. And the governments of our world secretly know this. But they don't want *you* to know. Too bad for them: The impenetrable veil of secrecy covering this top-secret menagerie or Pandora's Box of infernal beasts is finally about to be torn in two. What terrors lurk behind this veil, what is about to come crawling, soaring, pouncing, and rampaging out of that same menagerie, may shock you to your very core. Read on—if you dare!

~

Author's Note: Rather than compiling the chapters of this book by subject, I have elected to take a chronological approach. I did this because so much of this government interest in strange creatures was prompted by historic, world events such as WWII and the Cold War. With that in mind, I felt it most illustrative and helpful to outline the ways in which such clandestine research has developed, changed, and adapted, just as the world in which we live has done.

CHAPTER 1

THE PRESIDENT'S BIGFOOT

Given that we have to start somewhere on our search for the truth about monsters and officialdom, we might as well show a fair degree of ambition and aim just about as high as we can. And it doesn't get much higher than the office of the President of the United States of America. Theodore "Teddy" Roosevelt served as the Commander in Chief from 1901 to 1909 and is, to date, the youngest person to have ever held the position of presidential office: He was only 42 when he came to power. But, it's not the man's politics or youth that we're focusing on here. Rather, it's something monstrous, something malignant, something—or some *thing*—in the woods. Indeed, an inquiry into the controversial affair in question strongly suggests that the president became the recipient of nothing less than an early and quite graphic account of a violent encounter with a marauding, bloodthirsty Bigfoot.

As Roosevelt noted, frontiersmen are hardly the sort of people to be influenced by tales of paranormal or unexplained events. They are, after all, much too busy focusing on the practicalities and the day-to-day activities that go along with working, living, and hopefully surviving in the wild. But, there are occasional exceptions to that rule. And it was one of these exceptions that was actually made

President Theodore Roosevelt: A chronicler of Bigfoot? © George Grantham Baine, 1885. Source: Wikipedia

known to a U.S. president. The strange and sinister tale in question came to Roosevelt from a hunter by the name of Bauman. He had spent his entire life living and hunting in the American wilderness, and he was said to possess a profound knowledge of all sorts of tales of spectral entities and beasts of a most evil nature that haunted the forests, and that taunted and terrorized those people who dared intrude upon their dark domain.

Not surprisingly, given the impressive amount of time he spent in the forests of the United States, as well as his deep knowledge of supernatural lore, when Bauman spoke, the president listened. And he listened very carefully and closely, too. There was a good reason why Roosevelt's interest was so piqued. He, too, was an avid outdoorsman and a keen hunter. For example, in March of 1909, after his presidency was over, Roosevelt headed off to the expansive wilds of Africa, where he took part in a mammoth-sized hunt that saw at least 11,000 wild animals, including rhinos and elephants, slaughtered or captured by Roosevelt and his colleagues. So perhaps we can understand why Bauman's tale of terror so gripped the mind and imagination of this adventurous American president.

DEEP IN THE WOODS, A NIGHTMARE BEGINS

Back in the mid-1800s, Bauman and a friend spent time camping deep in the heart of the Bitterroot Range, a huge range in the Rocky Mountains that runs for more than 3,000 miles from British Columbia to New Mexico. It was on this particular range that something terrible, savage, and murderous lurked and roamed. At the time the incident took place, Roosevelt explained, Bauman was still very much a young man, and was hunting with a friend in a wild, mountainous area of the range. Not having had much success catching anything of significance, however, the duo elected to head to a much more desolate and seldom-traveled pass, through which ran a small stream, the home to a sizeable colony of beavers. Interestingly, the pass in question had developed an unnerving reputation as a place of malignancy and negativity. The reason for this was simple: Barely a year before the event that Bauman was about to describe, a woodsman was ripped to shreds and partially devoured by an unknown predator. The man's remains had been found by a shocked group of prospectors seeking their fortune, but who instead only encountered violent death and stark tragedy.

Bauman and his friend, however—both experienced men of the forests—were not at all daunted or dissuaded by this unsettling affair; in fact, far from it. The pair had packed all of the provisions they would need for significant time spent in the woods. Once they reached the pass, they headed still further up into the mountains with a pair of pack ponies as their only traveling companions. When the ground made going so difficult for the animals, Bauman and his buddy were forced to leave them in a stretch of meadow. The pair was now completely alone. For around four hours they trekked ever onward and upward through the dense, dark forest, finally reaching a small glade where they chose to make camp for the night—primarily due to the fact that there was evidence of plenty of game in the area. The next couple of hours were taken up with building a shelter and heading upstream to catch a few tasty salmon for a much-needed, hearty supper. It was when they returned to the camp that things took a decidedly alarming turn.

The camp was in a state of chaotic disarray. Some form of crazed, wild animal had evidently found the camp and virtually destroyed it. Their lean-to was mangled to pieces, backpacks had been torn open and their contents rifled, food was gone, and large paw-prints could be seen all around the area. The aggravated pair assumed they were bear prints—not an uncommon sight in that part of the world—so they had no choice but to quickly rebuild and settle down for the evening. As the night progressed, and as they scanned the area intently and with understandable trepidation, it became clear that the bear theory was not quite as sound as it had seemed earlier.

After carefully examining the numerous tracks, Bauman's comrade noted with astonishment that the beast—whatever it was—*had clearly been walking on two legs*. Totally baffled, the two studied the prints for a while longer, but were only able to conclude that they showed distinct paws or feet—but they were from no bear. The reason they knew is that although the tracks did seem to display evidence of claws—which certainly *could* have implied that a bear was the culprit, after all—bears only ambulate on their hind legs for very short periods of time. This particular creature appeared to be using them exclusively.

There was nothing more that could be done that evening, aside from getting a fitful night's sleep, which they did—for a while. Right around the witching hour, at 12 midnight, Bauman was abruptly jolted from his slumber and sat bolt upright. Although darkness was everywhere, his nose immediately told him there was an unclean wild beast lurking nearby. The animalistic stench was as strong and gut-wrenching as it was undeniable and immediate. But that was nothing compared to what happened next. Roosevelt listened, utterly transfixed and horrified, as Bauman described how a massive, animal-like form suddenly and briefly loomed into view. When Bauman had the firm presence of mind to quickly discharge his rifle in its direction, the beast made off like a shot. Unfortunately, the impenetrable darkness prevented Bauman from getting a good look at the elusive monstrosity in their midst. Not surprisingly, very little further slumber was had that night, and the pair wisely chose to get the campfire going again, in hopes of deterring the beast from returning and causing even more mayhem.

Fortunately, nothing else of an alarming nature occurred that night, and so the following morning, the two hunters headed off to check on several traps they had set the day before. Pleased with the plentiful bounty they yielded, the two headed back to the camp with several unlucky animals destined to become their tasty evening meal. But once again, all was not as it should have been. To the anger and growing alarm of the duo, their camp had been wrecked yet again. The newly reconstructed shelter was destroyed, their makeshift beds were in violent disarray and had been tossed around the glade, and just about everywhere there were those huge, bipedal footprints.

Unfortunately for Bauman and his friend, whatever had made those prints was quick to return. Although the darkness was by now all-encompassing, the cumbersome yet quick movements of the obviously very heavy animal on the floor of the forest echoed all around the camp, as did an unsettlingly weird, drawn-out howl or moan, which set their hair standing on end. Thankfully, the blazing fire kept the beast at bay. Bauman may have been an experienced man of the forest, but by now, even he had had just about enough, and so had his friend. Admitting to the president that the creature or fiend—whatever it was—had gotten the better of them, they decided that the wisest course of action was to get the hell out of there. Doing so in complete darkness would not have been the brightest of ideas, however; so the plan was to keep the fire going steadily through the night, which would hopefully deter the creature from coming any closer, and then make good their escape at daybreak. If only it had been that simple. Sadly, it was anything but.

Murder at the hands of a beast

When the sun began to rise the next morning, the two decided it was a case of now or never, and began their journey home. Ominously, however, even as they left the camp, the pair had a growing, nerve-jangling sensation that they were being shadowed by someone or something that, although it could be heard, quite clearly did not wish to be seen. The telltale, constant snapping of branches and rustling among the trees made it clear that the infernal thing was stealthily and expertly following their every move. This continued for the greater part of the day. As much as they wanted to beat a hasty retreat from that malevolent, godforsaken place, there was one last task the men needed to take care of: They needed food. On the previous day they had laid three beaver traps in a small pond situated in a large ravine. If the traps had worked, that meant yet another good supply of food for the return journey. In the heart of the dense forests, far away from home and civilization, food, of course, was a vital necessity. So Bauman volunteered to go and check the traps. It was a decision that may very well have saved his life. But his friend, who was tasked to set up their next camp, was not so lucky. Unfortunately, there was just no way the two could complete the journey back down the mountains before darkness fell.

Sure enough, the traps had done their job, and Bauman was a satisfied and very relieved man as he headed back to the camp. Satisfaction and relief were quickly replaced by fear, however. Very oddly, as the man himself explained to Roosevelt, as he reached the camp it was utterly and deafeningly silent. No birds, no animals, no wind, no noise. Even the soles of his shoes seemed to make no sound at all as they crunched on the fallen twigs and leaves beneath. This was most assuredly not a good sign. Approaching tentatively and with great caution, Bauman called out to his friend. There was no answer. That was even worse. With quickly mounting concern, Bauman could see that the campfire had all but gone out; the only thing that remained was its leftover smoke coiling and swirling upward into the thick forest canopy. By now extremely worried, Bauman called out to his friend with anxiety once more. Again, there was no reply.

Suddenly and most horribly, Bauman knew why his cries had remained unanswered. Stretched out next to the huge trunk of a once-mighty fallen spruce was what remained of the body of Bauman's hunting partner. Throwing all caution to the wind, he raced over to his friend to try to help, but it was obviously far too late. Bauman stared in utter shock as cold fear sank its teeth into him: The man's neck had been broken, and savage bite marks covered his bloodied, pummelled neck. And all around, there were yet more of those strange, huge bipedal tracks. Looking at the scene in a state of shock, Bauman had an all-too-clear picture of what had happened: His friend had evidently been sitting on the fallen spruce, warming his chilled hands over the welcoming fire that he had built right in front of it, when the unknown infernal beast of the forest had silently crept upon him from behind and mercilessly torn into him with pulverizing, almost-demonic force. What was worse, the broken body appeared as though the gigantic animal had rolled over it time and time again, apparently in some nightmarish form of obscene, maniacal glee.

Bauman, by now in a state of sheer panic, knew there was only one option available to him if he was to get out of there alive. He abandoned all his possessions and provisions, aside from his rifle, and ran for his life. It was a long and torturous trek back to civilization, during which, as Bauman told Roosevelt, he had come to believe that the creature was less flesh and blood and more diabolical or demonic, something akin to a terrible devil or goblin. Finally Bauman reached the pass where he and his friend had left the ponies; to Bauman's eternal relief, the animals were still there, happily grazing. It was a warming sight for Bauman, and the darkness and inchoate terror that had plagued him as he fled the woods finally lifted. The terrible events were at their end and the nightmare was over.

What we seem to have here is an undeniably fascinating and controversial tale that, rather incredibly, involves nothing less than a U.S. president being informed of the startling facts pertaining to an early, documented encounter with a violent, homicidal Bigfoot—an encounter that ended in the inhumane, bloody slaughter of a real person. Moreover, as will become graphically clear later in the pages of this book, this is not the only occasion upon which senior figures in American official-dom and hairy, giant man-beasts of the woods have crossed paths. For those reasons alone, the saga of President Theodore "Teddy" Roosevelt and his friend Bauman is an illustrative and, for our purposes, appropriate place to begin our turbulent journey into weird waters. And speaking of weird waters...

CHAPTER 2

SERPENTS OF THE HIGH SEAS

Who would ever have thought that sensational secrets about gigantic monsters of the seas could be contained deep within the concrete confines of a government facility in southwest London for more than a century and with nary an acknowledgment of their existence? This statement is one 100-percent true all the same, though. The location at issue is the National Archives, which is home to priceless, historic official documents dating back more than 1,000 years, as well as to millions of pages of previously classified files from the British equivalent of the CIA (referred to as MI6), the nation's version of the FBI (known as MI5), and the British Army, Royal Air Force, and Royal Navy. And it's to that latter body—those brave mariners of the mighty, high seas—that we will now turn our attentions. It's time to open up something undeniably remarkable: the British government's sea serpent file.

Monsters of the high seas (1734). Source: Wikipedia

"It is enough to frighten the strong at heart"

The dossier in question begins with a remarkable confrontation that occurred on May 9, 1830, between a gargantuan sea monster and the entire crew of the *Rob Roy*, which was a British Royal Navy ship that was on its way home after an extensive voyage across the perilous waters of the Atlantic Ocean. As the ship passed by the island of St. Helena, something incredible occurred, as the *Rob Roy's* captain, one James Stockdale, detailed in the ship's log. It was an astonishing event, worthy of the most sensational parts of Michael Crichton's *Jurassic Park* and Sir Arthur Conan Doyle's *The Lost World*:

> *About five p.m. all at once while I was walking on the poop, my attention was drawn to the water on the port bow by a scuffling noise. Likewise all the watch on deck*

were drawn to it. Judge my amazement when what should stare us all in the face as if not knowing whether to come over the deck or to go around the stern—but the great big sea snake! Now I have heard of the fellow before—and I have killed snakes twenty-four feet long in the straits of Malaca, but they would go in his mouth. I think he must have been asleep for we were going along very softly two knots an hour, and he seemed as much alarmed as we were—and all taken aback for about fifteen seconds. But he soon was underway and, when fairly off, his head was square with our topsail and his tail was square with the foremast (Stockdale, 1830).

Captain Stockdale continued on with his incredible account, and made a noteworthy observation that graphically demonstrated the sheer, astonishing size of the mighty leviathan that loomed large from the churning waves, one that could very likely have had Godzilla himself quaking in his reptilian boots:

My ship is 171 feet long overall—and the foremast is 42 feet from the stern which would make the monster about 129 feet long. If I had not seen it I could not have believed it but there was no mistake or doubt of its length—for the brute was so close I could even smell his nasty fishy smell. When underway he carried his head about six feet out of water—with a fin between the shoulders about two feet long. I think he was swimming about five miles an hour— for I watched him from the topsail yard till I lost sight of him in about fifty minutes (Ibid.).

Quite possibly still in a state of deep shock and awe when he prepared his official report on the monstrous encounter, Captain

Stockdale signed off in ominous and memorable fashion: "I hope never to see him more. It is enough to frighten the strong at heart" (Ibid.) Very few would ever disagree with those words!

"HE MUST HAVE BEEN OVER TWO HUNDRED FEET LONG"

A second 19th-century report of a sea serpent sighting that has been declassified at an official level by the British government details a December 13, 1857 encounter that, rather notably, *also* occurred in the vicinity of the island of St. Helena. And it was no less amazing than that of the *Rob Roy* of some 27 years earlier. A statement prepared by Commander George Henry Harrington revealed the notable facts to a concerned and worried British Admiralty:

> *While myself and officers were standing on the lee side of the poop—looking toward the island—we were startled by the sight of a huge marine animal which reared its head out of the water within twenty yards of the ship—when it suddenly disappeared for about half a minute and then made a reappearance in the same manner again—showing us its neck and head about ten or twenty feet out of the water. Its head was shaped like a long buoy—and I should suppose the diameter to have been seven or eight feet in the largest part with a kind of scroll or ruff encircling it about two feet from the top. The water was discolored for several hundred feet from the head, so much so that on its first appearance my impression was that the ship was in broken waters, produced, as I supposed, by some volcanic agency, since I passed the island before* (Harrington, 1857).

Captain Harrington had far more to impart. All of his statements suggested the presence in the waters of a beast whose incredible size would have put even an average-sized New York high-rise to shame:

> But the second appearance completely dispelled those fears and assured us that it was a monster of extraordinary length and appeared to be moving slowly towards the land. The ship was going too fast to enable us to reach the masthead in time to form a correct estimate of this extreme length—but from what we saw from the deck we conclude that he must have been over two hundred feet long. The Boatswain and several of the crew, who observed it from the forecastle, state that it was more than double the length of the ship, in which case it must have been five hundred feet (Ibid.).

The captain concluded in his official report: "I am convinced that it belonged to the serpent tribe." On that point, there seems to be very little doubt at all!

THE GREAT SEA SERPENT—AGAIN

Perhaps equally intriguing, not only was the British Admiralty carefully securing and studying reports of sea serpents from its very own sailors, but it was regularly scrutinizing both British and overseas newspapers for such accounts, too. While the precise reason for such an activity remains mysteriously unknown—perhaps it was lost to the inevitable fog of time or is still considered a classified matter by officialdom—it must be said that for the Admiralty to engage in such painstaking research is evidence that its interest in the phenomenon was far from cursory.

As one prime example of more than two dozen news clippings in the file, an article titled "The Great Sea Serpent Again," which had been extracted from a newspaper whose name the Admiralty's archives do not identify, states in part: "All doubts may be set at rest about the Great Sea Serpent. On the 6th of May 1863 the African Royal Mail steamer *Athenian*, on her passage from Tenerife to Bathhurst, fell in with one." The article continues that one John Chapple, the ship's quartermaster, was the first to see the huge creature, and described it as being around roughly 100 feet long, dark brown, and with its tail projecting up out of the water. Interestingly, the animal was described by Chapple as having atop its head "something like a mane"—a notable feature that has been reported for centuries in numerous sea serpent encounters all across the globe. The matter remained and still remains a mystery, carefully filed and preserved by Admiralty staff tasked with studying all matters beastly (National Archives file: HO 199/480).

Now that we have glimpsed some sea serpents, ships, and sailors of Britain's Admiralty, it's time for us to go back to terra firma and head off to Russia and a series of terrible experiments designed to meld man and ape into one unholy, infernal form.

CHAPTER 3

AN ARMY OF MANIMALS

In late 2005, a startling story reminiscent of the movie *Planet of the Apes* surfaced in the pages of a Scotland, United Kingdom newspaper called, appropriately enough, the *Scotsman*. The controversial feature in question described how formerly classified official documentation—which had reportedly been brought to the attention of the newspaper's staff—told of a shocking and secret history that easily rivaled, if not eclipsed the wildest of all science fiction sagas possible.

It was a strange and convoluted tale of how, in the 1920s and under the ruthless rule of the infamous Joseph Stalin, the Soviets planned to create an unstoppable army of terrible, powerful monsters that could be unleashed upon the battlefield against Russia's foes: a fighting force of nothing less than ape men, creatures with the physical strength of fully grown gorillas and the killer instinct of trained soldiers. Any brainpower beyond an inexorable instinct to slaughter the enemy *en masse* was, for obvious reasons, something that Stalin desired to keep to an absolute bare minimum. It was a program as ambitious as it was abominable. Stalin placed it in the hands of a man named Ilya Ivanov, a brilliant Russian physiologist with a flair for forward thinking in the worlds of cutting-edge science and zoology. As for the undeniably sensational story that appeared in the *Scotsman*, it was soon disseminated around the globe. It was picked up by such respected publications as the *New Scientist*, *Scientific American*, and the *New York Times*, and even became the subject of an episode of the History Channel's hugely popular cryptozoology-themed series, *MonsterQuest*. But was there any truth to the tale of Stalin's "mutant ape army," as the UK's tabloid newspaper the *Sun* dubbed it in eye-catching and sensational fashion? Here's where things get really murky (Starkey, 2007).

FACT, FICTION, AND HUMAN-APE HYBRIDS

That Ilya Ivanov would have been the ideal person to have had on board for just such a program is not a matter of any doubt, for one specific reason: Rather remarkably, Ivanov did indeed embark upon a controversial project to try to fuse ape and human into one foul creation. But, of critical importance is the matter of whether or not this was just as a result of his own particular and peculiar brand of controversial research, or if it really was at the stern orders of Joseph Stalin and the Soviet government, as a means to get the alleged official, secret project off the ground and create the most fearsome and powerful army that the world had ever seen.

Back at the turn of the 20th century, Ivanov established the very first center designed to cater to in-depth research in the field of artificial insemination in race-horses. The reasoning was obvious: to continue refining the bloodline until the ultimate horse in terms of speed, agility, and muscle power was perfected. Ivanov had also attempted to breed horses with zebras, albeit without even a modicum of success. Nevertheless, he was an undeniably brilliant scientist, and that meant a great deal to the Soviets, to the point where the Soviet Union's Academy of Science elected to fund his unique brand of work. It was funding, to the tune of approximately $200,000 in today's economy, to permit Ivanov to work on a plan to determine if ape-human hybrids could be brought to fruition, or if the entire matter was beyond both science and the laws of nature. We now know that humans and chimpanzees have a DNA sequence that is 95-percent identical, and coding DNA sequences that match to a figure of 95 percent. Therefore, perhaps we can never be fully certain that all attempts to splice man and ape were destined to end in failure.

Ivanov's first major port of call was French West Africa—more specifically, a research facility of the Paris, France–based Pasteur Institute in Kindia, French Guinea—where he arranged for the capture of a number of female chimpanzees, all of which were impregnated with sperm donated by human males. Far more controversially, Ivanov, electing to go down an avenue of truly dark proportions, also arranged for a number of local tribeswomen to be impregnated with sperm extracted from male chimpanzees. Utter failure was the only result, which, with the benefit of hindsight, is probably a very good thing for everyone concerned, particularly those tribeswomen, who were hardly willing participants in the sorry affair. Far from being dissuaded by the lack of success, Ivanov then decided to use gorillas instead of chimpanzees in his madcap scheme. No luck there, either. So, having achieved nothing of any significance in West Africa, Ivanov quickly returned to his native Russia. But he was still not done with his plans to combine ape and man as one. In fact, he was *far* from it.

Laboratories not unlike the one established in West Africa were quickly built in several locations, including Georgia, the birthplace of Joseph Stalin. These later experiments, from 1928 to 1929, focused on attempts to make apes pregnant with human sperm, and human females with ape sperm, just as was the case in West Africa. Once again, it was all a complete disaster. The project was finally abandoned once the Soviet Academy of Science got the message that it was simply not going to work. As for Ivanov, he was now *persona non grata* in his homeland. On New Year's Eve in 1930, he was arrested and sentenced to five years in jail, which was shortly thereafter commuted to five years of exile in Almaty, the former capital of Kazakhstan, where he died in 1932. Yet, evidence of the bizarre project remained in existence for decades. Just a few years ago, a group of workmen building a play area for children in the Georgian Black Sea town of Sukhumi stumbled across a crumbling old, underground lab where some of the diabolical experimentation had been undertaken all those years earlier. The telltale proof: a large number of ape skeletons scattered across the old stone floors of Ivanov's Dr. Frankenstein–like lab.

STALIN'S ARMY OF APE-MEN?

As we have seen, there's no doubt that Ilya Ivanov was putting forth a Herculean effort researching the feasibility of creating human-ape hybrids. History has demonstrated that to be the case. And there's also no doubt that the funding for this program—both in Russia and in French West Africa—came directly from the highest echelons of the Soviet Academy of Sciences. But did Joseph Stalin have anything to do with this, as the 2005 story in the *Scotsman* sensationally suggested? Was he really the brains behind the entire matter? And if so, was his goal actually to have under his iron-fisted, ruthless command an army of man-beasts that would pave the way for the eventual Soviet domination of the entire planet? Here's where we face a problem, and it's a very big one, too.

Persistent and careful digging by the media has failed to find *any* evidence, from *any* source, supporting or even hinting at Stalin's connection to the affair. Indeed, Eric Michael Johnson, who holds a master's degree in evolutionary anthropology focusing on great ape behavioral ecology, and who has dug deeply into this particularly controversial affair, notes that there is not a single shred of data to support the assertion that Stalin ever made such statements regarding an army of ape-men to anyone. Moreover, nowhere in any existing papers, files, documents, notebooks, or diaries are there any references to Stalin either playing a role in or even having any knowledge of Ivanov's work. But, as those who believe that Stalin knew of or even orchestrated the affair rightly assert, that same paperwork *does* demonstrate that the operation gained at least some support from certain elements within the Bolshevik government. While that may seem to be a triumph for those who think Stalin masterminded this weird and unsettling operation, it is not. The available papers make it abundantly clear that the Bolsheviks were enthusiastically pushing Ivanov's work for one reason and one reason alone: His research into the potential similarities between humans and apes strongly supported the theories of Darwinism and evolution. Thus, in the collective mind of

Claims of half-human and half-ape creatures have long proliferated. © H. N. Hutchinson, J.W. Gregory, and R. Lydekker, 1900. Source: Wikipedia

the Bolshevik government, Ivanov was someone whose theorizing would hopefully help to obliterate religious beliefs and eradicate related theories concerning the origins of the human race, which was one of the chief goals of the religion-hating Bolsheviks. Creating an army of ape-men wasn't even in the cards for them.

What we have here, then, is a saga that has some truth to it, that describes very real attempts to create human-ape hybrids that *were* undertaken by the Soviet Union's scientific elite, that *were* funded by the Soviet Academy of Science, and that *did* have the support of the Bolshevik government. But, the *Scotsman's* yarn about Stalin's ape-army, says writer Brian Dunning, "was merely another in a long line of cases where a journalist fills a slow news day with a sensationalized and/or fictionalized version" of an old affair that was very different in nature, scope, and intent than the newspaper suggested to its readers (Dunning, 2010).

MONSTER FILES

However, additional claims having nothing to do with Ilya Ivanov or Joseph Stalin have been made to the effect that human-ape entities have been created and both lived and thrived, in one case right into the 21st century.

FROM JULIA TO OLIVER

Born in Mexico in 1834, Julia Pastrana was a woman afflicted by what is termed congenital, generalized hyper-trichosis—or, as it is more commonly known, wolf man syndrome. In extreme cases, this condition causes bizarre behavior and radical mood swings, as well as excessive hair growth on the face and body of the victim. People with the condition typically display a normal facial appearance and skull-structure beneath all that hair, but Julia Pastrana was noticeably and gruesomely different. Most unfortunately, and similar to many people with physical deformities in centuries past, Pastrana was forced to earn a meager living in so-called circus freak shows, where she was sensationally advertised as being half-human and half-ape. However, Pastrana's appearance gained her far more notoriety than many others with hypertrichosis who simply suffered from an overabundance of facial and body hair: She had double rows of teeth set within powerful, protruding jaws that resembled those of an ape or gorilla. Indeed, as the photograph on page 36 shows, she looked downright savage and animalistic. Even the renowned Charles Darwin likened her appearance to that of a gorilla. And the fact that, while on display at a Moscow, Russia circus in 1860, Pastrana gave birth to a daughter who looked equally as savage only inflamed the rumors of her possible non-human origins even further. Sadly, both mother and baby died quickly afterward. The matter of whether Julia

Pastrana was simply a woman suffering from an extraordinarily rare medical condition, or something far weirder, continues.

Then there is the saga of Oliver, a chimpanzee caught in the Congo in 1960 when he was about 2 years old by a pair of animal trainers named Frank and Janet Berger. As the chimp began to grow, mature, and mix with both his own kind and with humans, some suggested that Oliver might not be a chimpanzee, after all. Or, more correctly: that he might not be *just* a chimpanzee. Perhaps he was what has become known as a humanzee, a term created to describe a hybrid creature that is part-ape and part-human. That Oliver only ever walked on two legs and never used the knuckles of his forelimbs, that he clearly evidenced several key differences in his facial features that set him apart from other chimps, and that he preferred the company of human females to those of his own kind even made the Bergers wonder if Oliver might be a cross-breed. DNA tests undertaken in 1996, however, demonstrated that while Oliver certainly walked in a decidedly unusual fashion for a chimpanzee, displayed uncharacteristic social behavior, and looked somewhat different than others of his own species, Oliver was definitely all chimp. He died when he was in his mid-50s in June of 2012.

Lest you think this rather anticlimactic ending is, well, the end, we now come to what is quite possibly the most controversial matter of all in this winding and convoluted saga.

The Almasty: an Ivanov offshoot?

All across Central Asia, as far west as parts of Europe and as far east as Mongolia, reports have long proliferated of hairy creatures known as *Almas* or *Almasty*, which seem to be far more akin to men than they do apes, although they reputedly exhibit clear and undeniable characteristics of both. Opinion is divided as to what these beasts really are, or may be. It is tempting to theorize that they are surviving pockets of our closest relative—the *Neanderthal*—which supposedly died out in the later part of the Pleistocene epoch, more familiarly known as the Ice Age. Certainly, some researchers, most notably the late American anthropologist and cryptozoologist Professor Grover Krantz, concluded that the Almasty may well be true humans, nothing more than surviving remenants of Mesolithic hunter-gatherers, similar to but far more primitive than the aboriginal natives of the more obscure parts of South America and southeast Asia. There's yet another theory—namely that at least a few presumed Almasty may actually be of a very different nature and lineage. They may be the rare, successful examples of Ilya Ivanov's crazed experiments—products of his mad alchemy secretly banished to the wilderness of the Soviet Union where they lived out their miserable existence.

A MAN-MONSTER OF THE MOUNTAINS

As the Second World War was winding down to its final stages, one creature resembling the Almasty was encountered at very close quarters. The man we have to thank for bringing the story to our attention was one Erjib Koshokoyev, who lived in the Caucasus Mountains (where the amazing incident took place) at the time, and who had heard stories of the hairy creatures of the hills and woods for a number of years prior. It was late one dark, autumn night in 1944, and Koshokoyev, working as a policeman at the time, was part of a group of local men scouring the nearby fields and hills on horseback, and keeping a careful watch for any signs of Hitler's marauding armies closing in. Without warning, the horse of the man leading the band suddenly stopped in its tracks, flatly refusing to go any further, or simply unable to because of overwhelming fear. This was hardly surprising: Barely 20 feet in front of the shocked group stood a huge, dark, hair-covered animal not at all unlike our common conception of the North American Bigfoot.

Seemingly aware that it had been spotted, the beast shot away at an incredibly fast rate in the direction of a nearby shepherd's cabin. The men—terror stricken, one and all—wasted no time ensuring their rifles were trained on the ramshackle old cabin as they tentatively approached it. The idea, quickly outlined by the officer in charge, was to try to take the creature alive and only to kill it if all other scenarios failed. If it could be captured and transferred to military personnel at Nalchik, the capital city of Russia's Kabardino-Balkaria Republic, the officer reasoned, then answers to its identity might very well be forthcoming. So, an ambitious plan was quickly put into place.

Upon reaching the building, the men made a circle around it, and were about to throw the door wide open when the Almasty—apparently having developed a fair idea of what was afoot—bounded out of the shadows and, in a state of crazed frenzy, dashed back and forth in front of the cabin's door while growling unintelligibly and with a terrible look on its primitive, rage-filled face. The officers, surprisingly able to keep their wits about them, made a line and moved forward, careful step by careful step. Without warning the man-beast suddenly charged right at them, and those previously intact wits were utterly and immediately lost. The line broke, and the men frantically scrambled to get out of the way of the monster as it raced toward a nearby ravine and the darkness of thick woodland.

As the man-thing raced away and finally disappeared for good, Koshokoyev had the presence of mind to make careful note of its appearance, which was essentially that of a human male utterly covered in long, dark red hair. But that was not all: The creature was not naked, as one might have expected, given that many cryptozoologists consider the Almastys to be wild animals. Instead, it seemed to be clad in what appeared to be a torn old caftan. Somewhat interestingly, such caftans of the very type described by Koshokoyev were extremely popular in the very same parts of French West Africa where Ilya Ivanov had conducted his controversial ape experiments two decades previously. Ragged proof that some of Ivanov's experiments, against all possible odds, had actually worked? Maybe we should not totally bet against it.

A SOLDIER SPEAKS

A second and very similar similar story comes from Lt. Col. V.S. Karapetyan of the Soviet Army's Medical Service. For the last three months of 1941 his infantry battalion was based about 20 miles from Buynaksk, in the Republic of Dagestan, Russia (also home to the Caucasus Mountains, interestingly enough). One day while on duty, Karapetyan was approached by a local policeman who cryptically advised that a strange man had been caught in the mountains who was suspected of being a spy in disguise. Wondering what on earth this curiously worded statement meant, Karapetyan quickly agreed to come along and see the captive soul for himself—who, Karapetyan was also told, was being held prisoner in a cold shed, as he apparently could not abide heat. Matters were getting even stranger, thought Karapetyan.

When he finally arrived at the shed, Karapetyan suddenly realized why there was such an air of profound mystery and high strangeness about the man. He was, said Karapetyan, naked and barefoot, and covered in a coat of shaggy, dark brown hair. The only parts of the creature that were free of hair were the soles of its feet and the palms of its hands. Even the face was covered with a fine growth of downy hair. The primitive-looking man was also a giant compared to the local tribes-people of the area, standing lightly more than 6 feet tall, with powerful-looking arms and thick fingers. His eyes, however, betrayed no intelligence at all. They were, said Karapetyan, both dull and empty, and decidedly animal-like. Moreover, the proto-man ate nothing, drank nothing, and failed to respond even in the slightest when a soldier chose to put out his hand as a sign of friendship. Karapetyan was in somewhat of a quandary. After studying the beast closely for a while, he told the military unit that had captured it that this was no disguised person, but a wild human of some kind. Since this was now a matter that had no bearing on Karapetyan's work, he left. He heard nothing more of the hair-covered thing that he briefly encountered during the carnage of the Second World War.

Most cryptozoologists that have chosen to investigate the Almasty phenomenon in depth have concluded that, if real, the beasts most likely represent the very last vestiges of some form of ancient man, possibly even *Neanderthals*, or maybe even the leftovers of some human lineage that modern-day science knows absolutely nothing about. Perhaps we should not entirely rule out the theory that, against all of the odds and utterly flying in the face of Mother Nature, one or two of Ilya Ivanov's crazed 1920s experiments really worked, and that fearsome, half-human and

MONSTER FILES

half-ape beasts were indeed secretly birthed in some unholy underground laboratory.

Is it stretching the bounds of possibility to suggest that this may be exactly what occurred, and that at least a few of these tragic atrocities against nature were clandestinely banished to the wilds of the Soviet Union, only to be encountered two decades later, after having reached adulthood, by astonished military personnel who presumed them to be unknown apes or surviving relics of ancient man? You decide!

CHAPTER 4

A WARTIME WOLFMAN

Jonathan Downes—a man who fits Rubeus Hagrid of the *Harry Potter* movies to the proverbial tee—is the shaggy-haired and wild-bearded director of the British-based Center for Fortean Zoology (CFZ), one of the very few full-time groups in the world dedicated to the study and investigation of unknown animals such as Bigfoot, the Loch Ness Monster, the Abominable Snowman, and the infamous blood sucker of Puerto Rico, the Chupacabra. Operating out of a centuries-old, spacious stone house in the mysterious and atmospheric wilds of Devonshire, England—where, incidentally, Sherlock Holmes creator Sir Arthur Conan Doyle set his classic, creature-themed novel, *The Hound of the Baskervilles*—the CFZ has embarked on mystery-filled adventures to virtually every corner of the globe in hot pursuit of all things monstrous and terrifying.

And it's from Jon Downes that what is surely one of the strangest monster-themed tales of all comes. It's a story full of a multitude of twists and turns, not to mention deep conspiracy, classified government files, and Second World War–era secrecy and subterfuge, told to Downes back in the early 1980s when he was in his early 20s and working as a psychiatric nurse at Starcross Hospital, Devonshire. It is the story of an old man who happened to be one of the key players in the puzzle all those years earlier, and a tale of how and why a mysterious creature and the British military were forever and controversially intertwined. With that all said, let us now take a close and careful look at this emotional tale of people long gone, shadowy secrets, weighty stigma, and a war-torn era immersed in chaos and conflict.

Deep throat revelations of the
werewolf kind

In the early 1980s, the man whom Jonathan Downes came to know very well was an elderly and retired nursing officer in his 70s who had been spared military service because of his profession in the medical field, and had instead eagerly embraced a place in the Home Guard, a division of the British military created during the Second World War chiefly comprised of men who were too old or too young to fight in the regular army. This was his own personal opportunity to fight against the Nazis. It was obvious to Downes that those years had been the happiest of the nursing officer's life. The rest of the man's professional career was spent working at the hospital, and he intimated to Downes that he had found the increasing struggle with a moribund bureaucracy exponentially tedious. So, when he was offered early retirement, he was quite happy to spend the rest of his days fishing and propping up of the corner of the bar in his local pub. But now he had finally met someone—Downes—with whom he wanted to share something that he had been keeping to himself for decades.

According to Downes, on a number of occasions during the Second World War, captured German aircrews who had been shot down over South Devon and the English Channel by British anti-aircraft personnel, were temporarily held in a remote wing of Starcross Hospital—located roughly 10 miles from the city of Exeter—until they could be transferred to the prisoner of war camp located high above Starcross on the looming Haldon Hills, thus firmly setting the scene for the weirdness to follow. On one particular occasion, the Home Guard were searching for a fugitive German airman in the woods that still surround Powderham Castle, which is situated half a mile or so from Starcross Hospital and which was constructed between 1390 and 1420 by Sir Philip Courtenay. The band of men ventured into the deepest parts of the woods and were in careful pursuit of their quarry when they suddenly encountered what they initially believed was the fugitive running through the trees right in front of them. The leader shouted at him to stop, but, as Downes revealed, it was all to no avail.

The old man who told Downes the story was actually one of the Home Guards in question, and he explained that one member of the party had been a teacher in Germany before the war and could speak the language fluently. He, too, ordered the man to stop, in German, but the fugitive ignored him. In 1942 the war was not going well, at least as far as the British were concerned, and Home Guard units, especially those in rural areas, were desperately under-equipped. Most of the patrol were only armed with pitchforks, although one had a dilapidated shot-gun, and the captain who led the unit had his old WWI service revolver.

As the tale was told to Downes in the comfortable confines of an old local inn, if it had been a normal patrol there would only have been about half a dozen of them, but large parts of the city of Exeter had been leveled by successive waves of German bombers, and the opportunity for a population of a tiny village like Starcross to actually face the enemy on equal terms was an irresistible, and understandable, lure. According to Downes's informant, the Home Guard patrol had been augmented by a gang of villagers baying for blood and desperate for revenge against the attacking Nazis.

The captain was an educated fellow, and he had no intention of using force to capture the fugitive unless it was deemed to be absolutely necessary. The man with the shotgun—a local farmer who had lost two of his sons in the desperate weeks leading up to the Battle of Dunkirk—had no such compunction, however. He was also drunk. Shouting and cursing wildly in the direc-tion of the presumed fugitive airman, he raised his weapon and fired. The dark figure ahead of them let out a loud cry of agony and fell to the ground. The captain was furious, and immedi-ately placed the drunken farmer under arrest and confiscated his shotgun.

It was at this point, Downes notes, the entire group came to a shocking realization: The man who had just been felled by the irate farmer was far stranger than anything that could have come out of Nazi Germany. The party had run on toward what they thought was an injured German airman, but to their hor-ror they found that it was nothing of the sort. Instead of a mem-ber of Adolf Hitler's Luftwaffe, they found a naked man who looked to be probably in his early 20s. But this was no normal man. In additional to being caked in mud, he was covered head to foot in a thick coat of hair. Someone whispered fearfully that they had just killed a real-life werewolf. Cold fear and an eerie silence descended upon one and all in the wooded darkness. That a full, bright moon loomed overhead only heightened the atmosphere of dread.

A DEEP AND DARK COVER-UP BEGINS

You may very well ask what happened to the hairy man who was supposedly felled all those years ago in dark woods just outside the English city of Exeter. Of his source and his strange and sensational story, Downes states that, apparently, the badly injured hair-covered man (or werewolf) was taken to Starcross Hospital in the middle of the night, and all efforts were made to make him (or it) comfortable. Then, in the early hours of the following morning, an unmarked black van arrived, and two men dressed in military uniform and another wearing a long white coat manhandled the mysterious victim onto a stretcher, loaded him into the back of the van, and whisked him away to destinations unknown.

Downes elaborates that the man never heard anything else about the affair again. He did hint, however, that government authorities warned everybody involved in the affair to say nothing whatsoever to anyone, ever. And, when officialdom gave this sort of directive, Downes's source stressed, it most assuredly meant it. Thus, in the prevailing culture of secrecy and silence ("loose lips sink ships"), they all quickly agreed that keeping mum was the order of the day. It appears that Downes was the very first person to whom the old man had ever spoken about the incident, albeit in distinctly whispered and cautious tones, after four decades of staying utterly silent. The reason the man broke his silence at that particular time was because he had recently found out that 60 years of incessant smoking had taken their toll: He was doomed to die of lung cancer within the next year or two and wanted to clear his conscience, so to speak.

DOWNES GOES ON A MONSTER HUNT

Although the entire story of his shadowy source strained credulity, Jonathan Downes could not deny the fact that the man came across as utterly genuine and earnest. Sitting in the corner of the bar, puffing away on a cigarette and wheezing gently like a dilapidated old steam-engine, he had the unmistakable aura of somebody afflicted by incurable cancer. He told Downes of these extraordinary events in a matter-of-fact tone, as if he were recounting nothing stranger than the previous weekend's football results. Downes wondered: Did the old nursing officer remember the exact location where the shooting took place? And, if he did, would he be prepared to take the eager young monster seeker to the location? Downes posed these questions diffidently, but to his delight the old man said that yes, he did know the exact place where the shooting took place and that he would take Downes to it. There was no time like the present, the man said; and so, finishing off their beers, they went outside and walked carefully and tentatively toward the old grounds of the castle. Matters were about to be taken to a whole new and very strange level.

If you're ever traveling from Dawlish toward the city of Exeter, go through Starcross village. When you pass the Atmospheric Railway pub, continue on past the large car park on the right side of the road, but instead of following the main road 'round to the left toward Exeter, take the right-hand fork that is sign-posted to Powderham. Continue down this little road for about half a mile and then, on the left-hand side, you will see an expanse of deer park bordered by a wide ditch full of brackish water that acts as a moat. Just before you come to a railway bridge, the moat peters out. Although it may not be there now, back in 1982, when Downes conducted the interview, there was a convenient gap in the fence. This gap was apparently well-known to the local poaching community in the village, and it served as their primary entry point into the woods where Lord Courtenay and his family raised their pheasants. Downes and the old nursing officer wriggled through the gap in the fence to find themselves suddenly trespassing on the forbidden grounds of the ancient castle. Realizing that even on such a brightly moonlit night it would be virtually impossible to venture any further into the thick and decidedly uninviting woods, Downes and his aged, and now very sick, informant decided to turn around and carefully retrace their steps back to Starcross village. Downes says that as he was working for the next few days, he made arrangements to meet his companion in the pub once again the following weekend. This time, however, the atmosphere was distinctly different and, as Downes described it, even frosty.

Downes recalls how he rushed to the Atmospheric Railway to fulfill their tryst, eager to learn if there was anything else the doctor had remembered, or if he could suggest any additional leads or sources that might conceivably help Downes uncover more facts of the story. Sure enough, his friend of a few evenings prior was there, puffing away on a cigarette and drinking his customary pint of ale. However, something had changed dramatically in those few days. Downes tried to broach the subject of the mysterious, hairy wild man, but his aged source was clearly unwilling to talk about it anymore. The old man expressed his deep regret for having confided in Downes; but, he said, he had done so since it was clear to him that Downes had an honest and enthusiastic passion for mysteries and monsters, and so his desire to help had gotten the better of him. When reality had set in at the cold light of day, however, the doctor could not shake off the possibility that perhaps, even after all these years, someone in government or the military was still keeping a stealthy, close watch on those few surviving members of the Home Guard who knew the basics of the terrible secret. And if they were still watching, said the elderly nursing officer, he was fearful that they might actually call upon him and even issue more threats in his direction—or worse, such as the engineering of a tragic and fatal "accident."

Quite understandably, Downes had far more than a few thoughts and opinions regarding this distinct and abrupt about-face. Whether it was the intimation of the man's imminent demise, or just a memory of the promise that he had made way back in the 1940s, Downes never really knew. Regardless, in stark contrast to his verbosity of the previous meeting, now the man was absolutely adamant that he didn't want to talk about it anymore. Not surprisingly for someone whose cryptozoological pursuits were growing dramatically by the day, Downes just could not let the beastly matter drop. For a while it's fair to say that the whole thing became something of an obsession for the man who is, as of this writing, Britain's most famous seeker of strange creatures. By Downes's own admission, the whole affair utterly fascinated him. So, during the next few months he very cautiously and tactfully broached the subject of the hairy humanoid of Powderham woods with a number of the other elderly men who drank in the pub or hung out at the hospital's social club. None of them knew anything, or if they did, they certainly weren't willing to admit to anything, significant or otherwise. And some sad news was looming on the horizon, too, as Downs sadly recalled.

The months passed, and the old man who had told him of the events in Powderham woods during 1942 was admitted to the cancer ward at the Royal Devon and Exeter Hospital in Exeter. Downes visited him on a few occasions—the last time, just a couple of days before he died, which was shortly before Christmas in 1982. Downes smuggled him in a bottle of Guinness and sat at the end of his bed as his friend drank it with relish. In view of his condition, and because he truthfully didn't think that he could get anything else out of him—Downes refrained from asking his source anything further about an incident that he obviously and bitterly regretted having shared. The conversation turned to lighter matters, as Downes tried to put a smile on the old man's face. But by that time the end truly was nigh, and it was only a matter of days before he passed away. Downes was determined to pay his respects to his friend and attended the man's funeral. Sadly, Downes was one of only a mere handful of people who were there. Afterward, Downes was convinced that that would be the last he would ever hear of the 1942 incident and considered the case closed. How utterly wrong he turned out to be.

SECRET FILES ON THE LEGENDARY MAN-BEAST

Christmas came and went, and Downes intended to put the whole matter behind him, since it appeared that he had hit a proverbial brick wall and had no conceivable way of getting around it. As a new year began, however, matters changed dramatically and in ways that Downes could barely have conceived only weeks earlier. In the early part of 1983, Downes was assigned the task of going through many of the old and voluminous filing cabinets that held more than a century's worth of patient records at Starcross, and that had barely been touched in decades. This was, Downes explains, all a part of his ongoing training as a psychiatric nurse. Although he was supposed to be focused upon researching the distribution of different mental and physical handicaps that the patients at Starcross hospital had suffered from over the years, much to his surprise and amazement—as well as more than a bit of concern for his own safety—Downes found what he strongly came to suspect was the solution to the mystery of the hairy man of the Second World War.

Among some of the older and fading files, Downes found a number of documents referring to certain members of a very wealthy, noble local family that were permanent patients at the hospital in the 1910s and '20s. Downes admits that he does not feel totally comfortable revealing the identity of the family—or at least not yet, anyway. He is, however, willing to share the startling facts that he has uncovered. It appears that at least as far back as the 19th century, and perhaps even much earlier than that, a strong vein of mental illness ran through the family. Far more significantly, a number of rare metabolic disorders were in clear evidence, as well. And it is in relation to this latter point that Downes comes to the meat of the tale, and possibly the origin of the hairy werewolf of Starcross Hospital.

The files contained the medical details of a number of the family's members, several of whom suffered from hypertrichosis, the same condition that afflicted Julia Pastrana. Because the condition is genetic, it seemed quite probable to Downes that the strain of hypertrichosis had not died out in the early years of the 20th century, with those held at the hospital who were afflicted by it and whose files he was able to peruse. Instead, the condition had persisted. As the years progressed, it seems that far more enlightened members of the family

The startling effects of Hypertrichosis. © Barnum & Bailey, 1921. Source: Wikipedia

decided to treat the next generation of these poor unfortunates at home, rather than subject them to the depressing monotony of an institutionalized life in isolated hospital rooms. One of those souls included the unlucky young man who was mistaken for a Nazi pilot in those darkened woods that fateful night back in the early 1940s.

Today, and with the benefit of 30 years of careful study into the story, Downes considers it quite likely that the unruly rabble that had accompanied the Home Guard on that night in 1942 had actually shot a member of the local ruling family, in the mistaken belief that he was a German airman. If he was covered in hair, suffering from mental illness, had briefly escaped from the confines of the family home, and was running wild in the woods, then all of these factors, when taken together, would explain just about everything that occurred that night. And, as Downes notes quite rightly and logically, it would also explain why the whole affair had been shrouded in official secrecy all these years.

Thus ends the sad, enigmatic, and conspiracy-filled saga of the Starcross werewolf, the decades-old secret of a powerful family, an official cover-up, frightened citizens, a shadowy informant who had hidden the truth for decades, confidential medical files, and a young man—Jonathan Downes—who, more than three decades ago, found himself immersed in significant details of the affair. Perhaps one day we will know the full and unexpurgated truth of this intriguing conspiracy. Or perhaps, like so many tales of deep cover-up, it will forever languish in mystery, intrigue, and a closely guarded, locked filing cabinet marked "Top Secret."

CHAPTER 5

WEIRD AND WACKY WINGED WONDERS OF WAR

History has shown that when war breaks out, and chaos and carnage rule, government agencies often employ some decidedly novel technologies to defeat the enemy. More than a few of those technologies have involved our furry and feathered friends, but in ways so downright strange that they have been relegated to the world of legend and myth, when they're actually all too strangely true. One of these technologies, if you'll pardon the pun, is just plain batty.

TURNING A BAT INTO A LIVING BOMB

Shortly after the Japanese attack on Pearl Harbor in December 1941, an operation called Project Bat Bomb was secretly approved by President Franklin D. Roosevelt. It was just about as crazy as its name suggests; quite possibly, it was even crazier.

The brainchild of a dentist named Lytle S. Adams, a good friend of the first lady, Eleanor Roosevelt—which is how the idea for the scheme reached the intrigued president—the plan was to create sturdy bomb-casings that were to be dropped over Japan by high-flying American bombers. These bomb casings would unleash upon the cities, towns, and villages of the country a decidedly unusual and nightmarish cargo: thousands upon thousands of Mexican free-tailed bats. After the casings were parachuted out of the planes and opened during descent, the bats would then likely seek out the many roofs of the buildings in the area, make their collective way in, and roost, as they are wont to do.

These animals weren't typical bats, though, and certainly the United States wasn't planning on releasing the creatures into the skies over Japan in order to give them good homes in a new, faraway land. The plan was for each bat to have attached to its body a small incendiary device containing deadly napalm. Then, after the animals had been given time to find places to roost in countless Japanese homes, factories, and buildings—the construction of which, in many cases, involved highly flammable materials such as bamboo and paper—the napalm-packed devices would be triggered with a deadly result: All across the targeted area, fires would suddenly break out, and chaos would ensue as the Japanese struggled to combat the escalating infernos springing up everywhere. And not a single member of the American military—aside from those flying the aircraft to their designated targets—would ever have to go into battle.

On paper it all sounded fairly plausible, as undeniably batty schemes so often do. Putting matters into practice proved disastrous, however. In May 1943, attempts were made to carry out an experiment along these very lines on home territory, specifically, the

New Mexico–based Carlsbad Army Air Field Auxiliary Air Base. Unfortunately, after a number of fully armed bats were mistakenly released en masse, the result was nothing less than the immolation of the entire test range. This was hardly a promising start. But officialdom chose to press on nonetheless, even to the point where an entire Japanese village was replicated out at the secret

Strange animal experiments of the Second World War. © Ernst Haeckel, 1904. Source: Wikipedia

Dugway Proving Ground in Utah, where follow-up experiments were undertaken. By all accounts the subsequent experiments were a success, and the makeshift village was turned into a blazing wreck with astonishing speed.

But further problems surfaced. There were countless delays in perfecting the miniature technology that would have to be built for tens of thousands of bats. Additionally, a large supply of the creatures first had to be captured from deep within a series of Texas caves. Thus, growing research into the atomic bomb project was seen as a far better means of bringing Japan's military to a grinding halt than a bunch of bats ever could. And so, Project Bat Bomb was permanently shelved. More than 20 years later, however, the U.S. government secretly launched a second project that was to blend animal and machine into an even more chillingly hideous form, as we shall see in a later chapter. But first we need to take a look at some other strange animal experiments that were conducted during the Second World War.

BATTLE OF THE BIRDS

In 1999, Britain's intelligence agency, MI5, declassified into the public domain some fascinating papers. In these documents, higher-ups expressed grave concern during the height of WWII that Hitler and his cohorts were planning on taking the ingenious step of employing pigeons to ferry top-secret data to Nazi spies that were hiding out in Britain. According to the released files, MI5 had determined that the birds were being bred for espionage work in Holland and France, and that the "pigeon agents"—as they were amusingly dubbed by the British government—were believed to have bases in Paris, Lille, Angers, and Cherbourg. (No word, however, whether they were equipped with their very own little runways!)

With this incredible and potentially catastrophic information in hand, MI5 developed an ingenious plan: They chose to turn the tables on Hitler by training an elite band of falcons—called the Special Falconry Unit—to eliminate the pesky pigeon problem. The falcons were specifically trained to intercept and kill Hitler's feathered friends. The available evidence would seem to suggest that the operation was a success. It is decidedly curious, however, that with so much data pertaining to straightforward aerial battles between the Allies and the Nazis having been in the public domain for decades, we had to wait until 1999 to learn the facts surrounding one of the stranger aerial conflicts of the Second World War. But it wasn't just the Nazis and British military that were looking to use birds in warfare.

USING A PIGEON TO GUIDE A MISSILE

For certain factions of the U.S. official infrastructure of the Second World War, people were not always seen as capable of defeating the Axis powers, and so birds were brought into the mix to help things along. And just as the Nazis did, they chose pigeons. The bird-brained idea was born out of the undeniably subversive yet progressive mind of a man named Burrhus Frederic Skinner, an inventor, author, psychologist, and, from 1958 to 1974, professor of psychology at Harvard University. The wholly unimaginatively named Project Pigeon basically involved strapping one of the government's feathered pals into a guided missile and teaching it to constantly peck on the part of the screen that displayed imagery of the specific target to be destroyed (courtesy of a front-loaded camera filming the ground). In other words, instead of relying on ground control, the doomed bird would literally steer the missile to its intended target via the tapping of its beak.

Just like the exploding bat project, it all looked reasonable and even feasible when discussed in round-table format. It worked far less well in reality, however, despite receiving a fair-sized budget from the National Defense Research Committee. Exhibiting a kind of "aviary attention deficit disorder," the pigeons couldn't seem to keep their minds on the job (or the target), which resulted in fortunately unarmed missiles flying wildly and chaotically above the desert surface of some of Uncle Sam's most classified test ranges, slamming into the ground, and turning the poor pigeons into piles of charred feathers.

If bats and pigeons couldn't help Uncle Sam defeat its foes around the world, it was time for officialdom to think even further outside of the box. And officialdom did exactly that. A terrifying, robotic monster was lurking in the shadows, ready to be dramatically unleashed upon an unsuspecting population.

CHAPTER 6

HOW THE PENTAGON MADE A MONSTER

It was the evening of September 12, 1952 when all hell broke loose in and around the small West Virginia town of Flatwoods. Something foul and malignant paid the townsfolk a visit of the truly terrible kind. As of this writing, more than 60 years after chaos and calamity briefly ruled, the memory of that long-gone eve still provokes massive amounts of gossip, debate, wonder, and even terror for the approximately 350 people that currently call Flatwoods their home. That the controversial encounter occurred at the same time as a veritable armada of flying saucers was seen in the skies of the nation's capital only raised the controversy level even higher. Was some form of terrible, alien monster roaming around Flatwoods on that long-gone night? Or, incredibly, do we need to look to none other than the U.S. government for the answers? We're on a hunt for what the townsfolk officially refer to today as—no surprises here—the Flatwoods Monster.

While the U.S. Air Force was busying itself with numerous UFO sightings on the night in question, startled Flatwoods townsfolk were dealing with something very different, indeed: the apparent crash-landing of, well, something atop a hill on land that belonged to a local farmer named G. Bailey Fisher. Chief among the witnesses were a Mrs. Kathleen May, a National Guardsman named Eugene Lemon, and a group of nearly hyperventilating teenagers. The group tentatively headed out together to the darkness-cloaked scene of the action, where they suddenly encountered a fiery ball of light that loomed ominously on the hill and emitted an unknown noxious substance that severely irritated the eyes and noses of all those present.

But all of that was suddenly forgotten when something terrifying loomed into view from the shadows of the surrounding trees. It was not one of those archetypal small, skinny, black-eyed, large-headed aliens, called "Greys," that have become so deeply ingrained in the fervid collective imagination of popular culture. No, this creature was 12 feet tall, seemingly brightly illuminated from within, and had a head that appeared to be shrouded in some kind of cowl. One of the terrified witnesses said it resembled the spade symbol in a deck of playing cards. As a showering array of flashing, arcing lights surrounded the beast, its glowing, penetrating, fiery eyes seemed to be fixed in the direction of the group. Not surprisingly, as the monstrosity began to glide above the ground toward them, they fled for their lives down the hill.

Returning tentatively to the scene a few hours later, the group were mightily relieved to find the monster now gone, but to where, exactly, no one ever knew. As a result, an enduring legend was born: More than six decades ago, a behemoth from another world paid the small, otherwise-sleepy and innocuous town of Flatwoods a bone-chilling visit. Or did it? From within the once-secret files of the U.S. government we find a fantastically controversial story that suggests that the monster of Flatwoods may have been nothing less than a strange, perhaps even robotic creation of the American military. Sound bizarre? Well, that's exactly what it was.

The U.S. military secretly invents a monster

In 2010, the U.S. Air Force quietly declassified (via the terms of the Freedom of Information Act) an April 14, 1950 publication of the RAND Corporation bearing the title *The Exploitation of Superstitions for Purposes of Psychological Warfare*. Researched and prepared by a RAND employee named Jean M. Hungerford, who was under secret contract to the Air Force at the time, the document detailed the many and varied ways and means—some truly ingenious—that beliefs and superstitions relative to supernatural phenomena could be leveraged on the battlefield to frighten and hence weaken the enemy. One such curious caper of that era, carefully cited within the pages of the RAND report, involved the U.S. military spreading utterly false stories throughout the former Soviet Union that American troops regularly saw the Virgin Mary at the height of warfare, thus promulgating the idea that God was on the side of the land of the free. But what, you may well ask, does any of this have to do with the glowing-eyed beast that briefly haunted Flatwoods in September 1952? It is here that we finally get to the crux of that particularly fraught matter.

One particular item that Hungerford focused a great deal of her attention on was a book titled *Magic: Top Secret*. It was penned back in 1949 by a mysterious and controversial character named Jasper Maskelyne. Maskelyne was both a highly skilled magician and an employee of the British Army. His job during WWII was to come up with alternative ways and weapons with which to deceive and defeat the Nazis. That Maskelyne—who came across in the pages of his book very much like the character "Q" from the James Bond novels and movies—may have significantly exaggerated his wartime role for the readers of *Magic: Top Secret* suggests that his operations were not quite as exciting, or even as real, as he claimed them to be. But not for RAND, and certainly not for the U.S. Air Force, which practically hung upon Maskelyne's every word, particularly as it pertained to one very weird cloak-and-dagger operation.

According to Maskelyne, while fighting the Nazis in the mountains of Italy at the height of the War, the British Army came up with a brilliant but undeniably strange idea. They built what was essentially, in Maskelyne's very own words, "a gigantic scarecrow, about 12 feet high" that would "stagger forward under its own power and emit frightful flashes and bangs." The idea was to have those Italians who were not sympathetic to the Allies believe the strange contraption—complete with "great electric blue sparks jumping from it"—was none other than the devil himself, working hand in glove with the Brits in some terrible, Faustian pact to defeat the Axis powers (Maskelyne, 1949). The result: terror, chaos, and calamity broke out wherever and whenever the flashing creature made its unearthly appearance. Villagers that were hostile to the British locked themselves in their homes, thus giving Maskelyne and his colleagues a very good idea about how monstrous superstitions and devilish beliefs could significantly influence the tide of war. Fearful of going to hell for aiding Hitler's minions, those very same hostile Italian villagers closed ranks and thought twice about ever rendering aid to the Nazis again. The British government gained an advantage, the Nazis had suffered significant blows, and not a single shot from a rifle had to be fired—all thanks to a fabricated, mechanized Satan.

U. S. AIR FORCE

PROJECT RAND

RESEARCH MEMORANDUM

THE EXPLOITATION OF SUPERSTITIONS FOR
PURPOSES OF PSYCHOLOGICAL WARFARE (U)

Jean M. Hungerford

RM-365

ASTIA Document Number ATI 210637

14 April 1950

Assigned to

This is a working paper. It may be expanded, modified, or withdrawn at any time. The views, conclusions, and recommendations expressed herein do not necessarily reflect the official views or policies of the United States Air Force.

The RAND *Corporation*
1700 MAIN ST. · SANTA MONICA · CALIFORNIA

The Pentagon creates a monster. © U.S. Air Force, 1950. Source: U.S. Air Force, under the terms of the Freedom of Information Act

IT'S ALIVE!

Believe it or not, there are deep and undeniable parallels between the British Army's demonic caper and the events at Flatwoods that occurred less than a decade later. Both the UK military's scarecrow and the monster of the little West Virginia town were around 12 feet tall; both emitted bright, flashing lights and strange sparks that arced wildly into the air; and, perhaps most important of all, both were classic examples of how psychological warfare can help defeat an enemy. On this latter point, let's not forget that Jean M. Hungerford's RAND report was specifically prepared for psychological warfare planners in the U.S. Air Force, who took a great deal of interest in what the witnesses and the media were saying about the Flatwoods Monster and what they thought the creature was. Perhaps not surprisingly, the Air Force took a great deal of secret interest in the words of Jasper Maskelyne, too.

You'll recall that Maskelyne's escapades occurred in small, isolated areas that could have been easily and secretly monitored to see how effectively the ruses were working. Flatwoods, a town of fewer than 400 people even today, would have made just such an ideal location for the U.S. Air Force to test a similar device to Maskelyne's devil, and see how a monster could be "animated" and used to deceive and terrify. Doing this in a safe and secure environment such as Flatwoods would have provided the U.S. Air Force with plenty of food for thought about how such a weird weapon could be used against a superstitious or credulous enemy at the height of the Cold War—if such a monstrosity were ever needed, of course.

THE ISSUE OF THE ACE OF SPADES

Interestingly, the primary witnesses to the Flatwoods Monster described the creature as having a head that resembled the spade design on a playing card. It so happens that this particular motif has played a leading role in more than a few psychological warfare operations orchestrated by the American military. By way of an example, a May 10, 1967 document titled *Vietnam: PSYOP Directive: The Use of Superstitions in Psychological Operations in Vietnam* describes how U.S. military forces learned that certain factions of North Vietnamese military personnel were "deathly afraid" of the ace of spades card and perceived it as an "omen of death." The author of the document (whose name is excised from the declassified papers) continues that, with this information in hand, American soldiers became "psy-warriors" and, "with the assistance of playing card manufacturers, began leaving the ominous card in battle areas and on patrols into enemy-held territory." Interestingly, files also show that the U.S. military had clearly done its homework on this matter, and came to realize that the dread of the ace of spades on the part of certain factions of the Vietnamese military dated back to the 19th century, when French Catholic missionaries to Vietnam encountered the Montagnard people of Vietnam's Central Highlands and learned how the imagery provoked terror in the region (*Vietnam: PSYOP Directive: The Use of Superstitions in Psychological Operations in Vietnam*, 1967).

Two operations—one at Flatwoods, West Virginia and the other in Vietnam—that involved psychological warfare strategists in the U.S. military, two operations that involved the deployment of playing card motifs, and two operations that were designed to provoke fear in the individuals targeted. Do we really need further evidence that the Flatwoods monster was the creation of officialdom? Finally, how truly ironic it would be if the U.S. Air Force had taken its inspiration and ideas from Jasper Maskelyne, a man whose claims and assertions are viewed by many today through deeply suspicious eyes. Deceit, duplicity, and deception, it seems, are the common threads that run through virtually the entire tapestry of this particular saga of monstrous secrets.

Chapter 7

Welcome to the Jungle

The very real possibility that the diabolical "creature" of Flatwoods, West Virginia, was an ingenious, robotic creation of the U.S. military is further bolstered by the revelation that the Department of Defense (DOD) was engaged in yet *further* bizarre monster-making and myth-spreading during this exact same time frame. Indeed, while a glowing-eyed beast of the night was terrifying the good folk of Flatwoods, West Virginia, Pentagon scientists and psychological warfare planners within the American military were spreading dark tales of blood-sucking, monstrous vampires roaming the wild depths of the Philippines.

The truly fascinating saga was one born out of the fertile and fantastical mind of Major General Edward G. Lansdale. During the hostilities of WWII, Lansdale spent a great deal of time working with personnel attached to the U.S. Office of Strategic Services, with whom he carefully developed and nurtured

Major Edward Lansdale, the brains behind a monstrous vampire. © U.S. Air Force, 1963. Source: Wikipedia

his very own weird ways of defeating the enemy—in fact, just about *any* enemy. But it was when Lansdale was given a post-war assignment at HQ Air Forces Western Pacific in the Philippines that things really began to heat up and the strangeness rose to stratospheric levels.

At the specific insistence of the sixth president of the Philippines, Elpidio Rivera Quirino, Lansdale was brought in to work on a project of fantastic proportions with the Joint United States Military Assistance Group. The year, rather notably, was exactly the same as Flatwoods: 1952. As for the reason, it was to offer secret American military aid—by virtually any means necessary—and intelligence support in stamping out a growing uprising on the part of what were known as the Hukbalahap. During the Second World War, the Huks, as they came to be known, operated as guerilla units in the Philippines with just one goal in mind: to wipe out the invading forces of the empire of Japan. And they didn't do a bad job of it, either. But when the war finally came to an end in 1945, the Huks quickly turned their attentions toward ousting the government of the Philippines. From 1946 onward, face-to-face

Monster Files

confrontation between the Huks and the forces of the government and the military was commonplace. The time came, however, when enough was seen as being just about enough. Cue the stealthy entrance, stage left, of Major General Lansdale and his mysterious box of terrible tricks.

A BLOODSUCKER OF THE NIGHT

While deep in discussion with President Quirino and his staff about the varied ways and means available to defeat the Huks, Lansdale came to learn just how deeply influenced the latter were by certain local myths and legends. Lansdale had a sudden flash of brilliance: He decided to bring one of those same superstitions—the shape-shifting Aswang vampire—to life. The Aswangs were fearsome, bloodsucking monsters of gigantic proportions that were said to lurk deep within the jungles of the Philippines. As Lansdale learned to his profound interest, the Huks carefully and cautiously avoided any location where the predatory Aswangs were said to dwell and feast. Thus, an amazingly off-the-wall plan soon came to fruition. Decades after this previously classified operation was over, when he finally felt comfortable speaking out publicly, Lansdale himself had this to say on the controversial matter:

> To the superstitious, the Huk battleground was a haunted place filled with ghosts and eerie creatures. A combat psy-war squad was brought in. It planted stories among town residents of an Aswang living on the hill where the Huks were based. Two nights later, after giving the stories time to make their way up to the hill camp, the psy-war squad set up an ambush along the trail used by the Huks (Lansdale, 1991).

It was then that things were taken to a whole new, and almost unbelievable, level. Lansdale's men were suddenly transformed from elite soldiers of the U.S. military into predatory beasts of the dark forest, simply by means of the power of suggestion and a much-feared myth seemingly brought to life. On the first night of the operation, the elite team carefully and stealthily followed a Huk patrol on its regular evening check of the area. It was then, when the skies and woods were at their absolute darkest, that they were suddenly and silently attacked from behind. The last man on the patrol was quickly plucked from the group and his neck was punctured with a specially crafted lethal weapon that had been designed to mimic the classic calling card of the legendary bloodsuckers: two deep and savage wounds to the neck. But that was only the beginning. The team then tied a rope around the ankles of the victim, threw the other end of the rope over the thick branch of a nearby tree, and hauled the man's body into the air to let it hang there—upside down—for hours, as the blood slowly drained out of the vicious, gaping neck wounds. Then, with the dastardly deed finally complete, the body of the Huk was carefully taken down and quietly dumped near the camp of his rebel comrades. The result, as Edward Lansdale noted, was as amazing as it was swift:

> *When the Huks returned to look for the missing man and found their bloodless comrade, every member of the patrol believed that the Aswang had got him and that one of them would be next if they remained on that hill. When daylight came, the whole Huk squadron moved out of the vicinity* (Ibid.).

As a direct result of these actions, vitally important strategic ground was taken out of the hands of the Huk rebels.

That a bloodsucking monster was brought to life, and quickly and deeply influenced the outcome of a military engagement, despite the fact that the same monster never really existed in the first place, is without doubt extraordinary. And, in light of the data contained in this chapter, those who dearly wish, or fully believe, the monster of Flatwoods to have been an entity of unknown origins, and that bloodthirsty Aswangs really are among us, might do well to reconsider those particular views. While it may be said that both monsters "lived" in some strange way, the nature of their odd, brief lives was even stranger than it would have been had they actually been fantastic beasts of flesh and blood.

CHAPTER 8

ANIMAL ESP AND THE U.S. ARMY

According to formerly classified U.S. Army documents, in the early 1950s, a Dr. Joseph Banks Rhine, PhD, of Duke University, was quietly approached by senior personnel in the American military to participate in a program of truly extraordinary and mind-boggling proportions. The clandestine operation was designed to determine if dogs, cats, and pigeons possessed any significant degree of extrasensory perception (ESP). The reason was as bizarre as it was controversial: to train those very same animals to use their near-magical powers of the mind to locate enemy land mines buried beneath war-torn battlefields. As for why Rhine was chosen for this weird, *Lassie*–meets–*The X-Files* project, the answer is very simple: Prior to his secret work with the Army, Rhine was a noted, albeit controversial figure within the field of paranormal research. (Indeed, he later became known as the father of modern parapsychology. A prestigious title, certainly. Not only that; it was Rhine who coined the term *extrasensory perception*, thus forever establishing for himself legendary status as a leading player within the realm of psychic phenomena.)

To understand what it was that prompted the United States Army to embark upon its grand, strange scheme, we have to go all the way back to the 1920s, when Rhine secured a master's degree and a doctorate in botany at the University of Chicago and began digging into matters relative to alternative science. From there, it was all very much uphill: Soon thereafter Rhine accepted a position at Duke University and began pursuing in earnest his burgeoning passion for ESP and the mysterious powers of the mind—and not just human minds, but those of animals, too.

Rhine routinely used a pack of 25 Zener cards in his research. Named after their creator, Karl Zener, a psychologist who graduated from Harvard, taught at Princeton, and worked with the U.S. National Research Council, the cards display a variety of designs—lines, crosses, squares, and circles. In a typical experiment the goal was to sit two people opposite one another, and have one act as the sender and the other as the receiver. The "sender" would focus intently on the image displayed on the card in front of him, while the "receiver" would try to divine that same image via psychic means. Sometimes it worked and sometimes it didn't, but for Rhine, even if it yielded a low success rate, well, it was still a success. So, he pressed on with his work with even greater intensity and focus. As a testament to this, by the early 1940s, the number of trials that he and his staff embarked on had reached almost *one million*.

As a new decade progressed, and as Rhine's status, reputation, and (eventually) legend as a guru in psychic circles grew ever larger, it was not just his fellow parapsychologists, the general public, and the mainstream media that were looking at Rhine through interested and intrigued eyes. Little did Rhine suspect at the time that senior personnel behind the closed, cloaked doors of the Pentagon were doing exactly that, as well. They were hardly broadcasting that interest, however. Indeed, steps were taken to keep official interest in Rhine's work under secure wraps at all times, even when the man himself was carefully approached by government sources with the hopes of getting him onboard as a Cold War–era warrior of sorts.

DOGGEDLY LOOKING FOR MINES

It was a normal day in January, 1952—or as normal as any day can ever be for someone whose routine involved the study of psychic phenomena—when Rhine received in his office a telephone call of a kind that many might expect to see only in a Hollywood movie. A life-changing question was put to Rhine by the "Man in Black" at the other end of the line: Would he be interested in serving his country by heading up a classified project that could help save American lives and significantly strengthen U.S. national security, and all via psychic means, no less? Of course Rhine was interested! Thus began a most odd relationship between the psychic scientist and the top brass of the American military.

Having signed a lengthy and complex nondisclosure contract with the Army, Rhine was invited in February 1952 out to the Engineering Research and Development Laboratories of the Army's Virginia-based Fort Belvoir facility, where he was briefed on the ambitious scheme to turn animals into psychic spies and mine-detectors. Rhine was immediately hooked on

Psychic dogs of the military. © U.S. Army, circa 1960s/1970s. Source: Wikipedia

the new and novel idea, and work began in earnest. Within days, the Army provided Rhine with half a dozen young German shepherds that were to function as his test subjects for about three months.

Although the admittedly limited number of publicly available U.S. Army files on this matter do not fully describe how, exactly, Rhine and his cohorts tested the dogs' psychic powers, they do demonstrate that two dogs in particular scored high. Their names were Tessie and Binnie, and apparently they worked wonders locating dummy mines buried on remote stretches of California's sandy coastline in June of 1952. Rhine's own words, which were recorded on the same day of the initial experiment, are notable: "The success was high enough that it was soon evident that the dogs were alerting the mines before they set foot on the surface above them." And the Army's response was positively glowing, too: The result of the first day's total of 14 trials was 86 percent successful (Rhine, *Final Report for Contract*, 1953).

MONSTER FILES

Tessie and Binnie continued to yield very impressive results, so much so that the military quickly took things to another, far more ambitious level. They moved away from the beach and buried a number of deactivated mines under the water at distances of anywhere from 40 to 60 feet from the shore. When the paranormal pooches were brought to the beach shortly thereafter, they barked loudly, leaped out of the back of the vehicle, raced for the sea, and excitedly swam right to where the devices lay concealed below the churning waves. Rhine reported back to the Pentagon and got straight to the point: "There is at least no known way in which the dogs could have located the underwater mines except by extrasensory perception." The excited top brass didn't disagree. With Tessie and Binnie having quickly met with the Pentagon's approval, the military expanded its attention to include not just man's best friend, but also the arch enemy of that same best friend, the cat (Ibid.).

CURIOUS CATS AND PARANORMAL PIGEONS

Interestingly, much of the relevant data concerning how the several cats used in the program were taught to locate the mines remain classified under U.S. national security regulations. Nevertheless, we do have the following brief words from Rhine contained in the files, which make it clear that they predicted a successful outcome in this venture, as well: "Most of the things reported about dogs that suggested the possibility of ESP as a factor were also claimed for cats. Psychologically, the animals are close enough together to make a transfer of findings from one species to the other fairly likely." It's most regretful that the bulk of the cat-related files remain unreleased, since Rhine's statement that "a transfer of findings from one species to the other [was] fairly likely" appears to imply that plans were initiated to have the cats and dogs work together and actually combine their psychic skills to locate the mines—an undeniably extraordinary idea (Ibid.).

Raising the seriously weird stakes even higher, the Army also wanted to see what Rhine thought about getting a small army of psychically gifted pigeons along for the ride, too. Evidently, this proved to be overly ambitious and not at all successful, as Rhine himself admitted to the Army: "The mystery of pigeon-homing and the possibility that extrasensory perception enters into that performance led us to undertake the solution of the problem of how these pigeons find their way home. At the termination of the contract the problem had not been solved" (Ibid.). As Rhine was careful to stress with respect to the pigeon-based studies, however,

> researchers have ruled out all existing sensory hypotheses, thereby making extrasensory perception a more plausible interpretation than it has been hitherto. This research has opened up possibilities of importance not only within but far beyond the scope of the projects specifically dealt with. The problems raised on this project involve basic research that may remain in the category of the inapplicable for many years. Measured against this is the enormous value, not only to intelligence but to application in a wide range of military uses of extrasensory perception (Ibid.).

THE RESEARCH CONTINUES

If the enigmas of the animal brain could be used to locate land mines, then what else might they be capable of? The military clearly recognized the logic and full import of this question. But Pentagon staff had something else on their minds, too: Precisely how reliable *were* Rhine's tests? Could it not have just been the case, some sources within the Army began to speculate, that Tessie and Binnie were merely using their powerful sense of smell, rather than engaging any sort of paranormal talent, to find the mines? To his credit, Rhine did consider just such a possibility, and, as a direct result, both the tests and the attendant conditions were modified to make sure that Tessie and Binnie were not exposed to strong cross-winds that might have allowed the pair to uncover "chemical stimuli" from the mines. Again, this seemed not to affect their successes—not for some time, anyway (Ibid.).

Rather oddly, the positive results started to drop off dramatically in 1953, which led Rhine to advise his Army contacts that "the thing that stands out is that the ability that is being measured is a very elusive and delicate one" (Ibid.). Indeed, it was this statement that ultimately led the Army to make the decision to close down the program. Again, not because of the lack of any success: The Tessie and Binnie saga strongly suggested that they had achieved something new and notable here. The problem for the Pentagon was that this success was fleeting and uncontrollable; it could not be predicted, let alone guaranteed. And it was this somewhat-haphazard success rate—coupled with the fact that the military was still struggling to comprehend the realm of ESP—that led to the termination of the operation (Ibid.).

Rhine was far from being deterred, however. He continued with his research for decades afterward, and penned a number of books on the subject, including *New World of the Mind* and *Parapsychology Today*. Although he died in 1980, his legacy as a prime mover in the arena of ESP lives on. As for Tessie and Binnie, one has to wonder if their presumed, advanced mind-powers led them to realize, in some curiously canine fashion, that they were helping Uncle Sam's efforts to keep the United States safe from overseas enemies. Or perhaps the prospect of racing around Californian beaches under the hot, West Coast sun in the summer of 1952 was just a big lark for them, and they ultimately went to their graves sadly unaware of their brief, yet without a doubt significant, role in one of the U.S. government's strangest secret projects of all time.

CHAPTER 9

A YETI-HUNTING 007

Did the Central Intelligence Agency secretly encourage a famous pursuer of monsters to do its dark and dirty work for them in the 1950s? Is it possible that more than a few of this man's expeditions in search of the legendary Abominable Snowman of the Himalayas were nothing but ingenious cover stories to allow for clandestine espionage operations on nations that were potentially hostile to the United States? And what of this same character's untimely death in a plane crash that still provokes controversy to this very day, decades after it occurred? These and many other highly charged issues dominated the life and work of a fascinating and mysterious man named Tom Slick, a devotee of cryptozoology, an Indiana Jones–like adventurer, a figure with numerous links to the secret world of officialdom, and—just perhaps—the James Bond of the monster-hunting world.

A SEEKER OF STRANGE CREATURES

Born in San Antonio, Texas, in 1916, when the First World War was still raging, Thomas Baker Slick, Jr., was the son of one Thomas Baker Slick, Sr., who made a mountain of money in the oil business of the 1920s, and who became known as both the King of the Wildcatters and Lucky Tom. Fate demonstrated that Tom Slick's father wasn't so lucky in the end, however: He died in 1930 at the tragically young age of only 46. Slick may have lost a parent, but in doing so, he inherited a fortune of literally millions.

Just like his father, Tom Junior proved to be a mover and a shaker. During the Second World War, after having studied at Yale, Harvard, and MIT, Slick worked with the Washington, DC–based War Production Board as well as the Board of Economic Warfare, and served with the U.S. Navy in the Pacific theater. He was the brains behind three organizations that became known as the Texas Biomedical Research Institute, the Southwest Research Institute (the focus of which was on advancing technologies), and the Mind Science Foundation, which explored the mysterious potentials of the human brain. Slick was also a big fan of modern art, and an author with world peace firmly on his forever busy mind: In 1958 he published a book on this very matter, titled *Permanent Peace: A Check and Balance Plan*. And then there are those monsters that so fascinated him.

Rather interestingly, it seems that Tom Slick's passion for excursions of the wildlife variety was prompted by a 1928 expedition to China that the sons of President Theodore Roosevelt—Kermit and Theodore IV—embarked on, during which they hunted down and killed a giant Panda. As we saw in the first chapter of this book, Roosevelt Sr. himself was no stranger to cryptozoology, and he may very well have been the recipient of an early report of a predatory Bigfoot on the loose in the Pacific Northwest. This is interesting because, although Slick's interest in cryptozoology was wide-ranging, it was the legendary Abominable Snowman, or Yeti—so similar to the American Bigfoot—that attracted most of his attention. But before we get to the matter of Tom Slick's Yeti quest, let's first take a look at what the legendary beasts might actually be.

CASES, SIGHTINGS, AND THEORIES

Depending on who you care to ask, the Yeti is thought to be a giant ape of unclassified origins and nature, a surviving example of something long thought to be extinct, or an admixture of hoax, folklore, misidentification, and myth. In Tibetan, and particularly Nepalese culture, tales of a giant, Bigfoot-like creature existing centuries ago are still passed from generation to generation. The Rongkup people, for example, recount ancient tales of a mighty creature of the glaciers, a large and lumbering ape-like animal that used stones as weapons, and whose blood was occasionally used in religious ceremonies. In 1832 the story surfaced of a mountaineer and naturalist named Brian Houghton Hodgson, who exhibited a deep interest in Buddhist teachings and beliefs. That same story told of how a number of Hodgson's team encountered on the Himalayas a large, hairy animal that walked on two legs and that was clearly thought to be neither bear nor man. Hodgson, utterly baffled but admittedly fascinated, could only theorize that the creature was possibly an orangutan, or at least something along those lines. Similar reports would continue to surface, but it was not until 1921 that the appellation "Abominable Snowman" came into being.

In that year, Lieutenant-Colonel Charles Howard-Bury—a British politician and a soldier with the King's Royal Rifle Corps—led a team to the Himalayas called the Everest Reconnaissance Expedition. Its primary goal was to determine whether the northern side of the massive mountain might admit access to the peak. While mapping out the treacherous mountain at an altitude in excess of 20,000 feet, Howard-Bury and his team came across a set of surprisingly large footprints that appeared to resemble those of a barefooted man—certainly not something the group had anticipated encountering at those heights! A number of the local guides who had been hired to take part in the trek were later interviewed about their experiences by a journalist named Henry Newman (who wrote for the Calcutta-based *Statesman*). It was Newman who coined the term *Abominable Snowman*, after hearing of their knowledge of the legendary monster. It was almost certainly a mistranslation, however. The guides described the beast as being *metoh*, meaning "filthy," which Newman then misinterpreted to mean "abominable." And it was out of that error (or, as some suggest, that imaginative artistic license) that the creature's most famous name was introduced to a soon-to-be captivated world.

Interest in the mythological beast seemed to reach fever pitch in the 1950s, when a number of acclaimed mountain climbers, including Eric Shipton, Sir Edmund Hilary, and a team sponsored by Britain's *Daily Mail* newspaper, photographed what appeared to be gargantuan footprints in the frozen heights and collected sightings of the wild man-thing said to be in their midst. While public interest in and fascination with the Abominable Snowman is certainly nowhere near what it was decades ago, the hunt still goes steadily on.

One interesting candidate for what the animal/beast might really be is the *Gigantopithecus blacki*, a massive ape with an estimated height of around 10 feet and a weight in excess of 1,000 pounds. That these creatures lived and roamed across significantly sized portions of what are today Vietnam, China, and India makes the possibility that they are responsible for Yeti reports all the more intriguing. Expect for one problem, an impediment that is just about as big as the legendary Snowman itself: According to mainstream science, *Gigantopithecus blacki* is thought to have become extinct more than 100,000 years ago. On the other hand, nature is undeniably tenacious and very good at clinging on against all odds, perhaps even against accepted scientific wisdom. Thus, if *Gigantopithecus blacki* is not so extinct, after all, we may well have the perfect explanation for the Yeti in the form of an empirically verified huge ape that dwelled in the very same area where, thousands of years after its presumed extinction, people are still seeing huge, anomalous apelike creatures. With all of this as context, let us now return to the mystery-filled life and work of Tom Slick, the Yeti-hunter *par excellence*.

ON THE TRAIL OF THE UNKNOWN

Tom Slick was a man with a deep passion for travel, adventure, and exotic lands—all perfect and prime ingredients for becoming a cohort of the CIA in the 1950s. In 1956, for example, Slick was in Guyana on a diamond hunt when disaster struck, and his aircraft was forced to make an emergency landing. He ended up spending time with a local tribe for two weeks before finally being rescued. His only means of survival in the harsh, primitive environment was a diet of parrot meat. Then there was Slick's excitement-filled 1950s trip to New Zealand, the site of an ambitious hunt for wild boar. These are just a two examples of the man's many and varied escapades of the alternative and entertaining kind. But it was in relation to the Yeti that Slick really made, and left, his mark.

In 1956, Slick decided that Nepal was going to be next on his list of must-see places, and the Yeti was going to be his next creature of interest. And how was he going to find the mighty, lumbering man-ape of the huge and ancient mountains? With a helicopter and bloodhounds—what else? This was hardly well-received by local authorities, however, who immediately put a stop to Slick's plans. However, on March 17 of the following year, according to cryptozoologist Loren Coleman, an undeterred Tom Slick kicked things off in style in the Arun Valley, located in eastern Nepal.

During the next 48 hours, the Nepalese government made a public statement—intended for the media to disseminate widely—loudly warning all visiting adventurers and explorers that any attempts to snare, harm, or kill a Yeti would result in the wrath of officialdom coming down very hard on the culprit or culprits. Slick got the message, but that didn't deter him from roaming the mountains with a loaded gun. Nor did it prevent him and his team from taking along for the ride a number of steel traps in which to imprison a Yeti, in the event they were lucky enough to find and capture one. Although, one imagines it would not have been an easy task to try and entice a giant hairy ape into a cage it had no intention of entering!

Several expeditions were undertaken and funded by Slick in the late 1950s. His own, personal excursions, however, came to a sudden and life-changing halt when, on one such trip, the brakes failed on the vehicle that he and his team were driving through the treacherous mountains. One and all quickly leaped to safety, but for Slick the jump was a bad one: His knees were severely damaged; from then on he was forced to play the role of funder rather than participant. Nevertheless, Slick's time in Nepal had convinced him that the Yeti was a very real creature. When Slick began to expand his research to include the North American Bigfoot, his attitude toward the world's mysterious man-beasts began to change dramatically. The days of wanting to hunt down and kill such a creature were replaced by a desire to obtain definitive and irrefutable evidence in the form of photographs and then let the beasts live in peace and privacy. Sadly, as we will see later, Slick did not live to see his dreams and plans come to fruition.

TIBET IN TURMOIL

One of the most fascinating claims made about Tom Slick is that while he was legitimately searching for the Yeti in Tibet, he was also there at the request, or maybe even the order, of the CIA to keep a close and careful watch on the fraught relationship that existed between its population and the government of the People's Republic of China. History would seem to bear this out. Skirmishes between Tibetan rebels and Chinese armed forces in both the Amdo and Kham regions of Tibet dated back to 1956, only months before Slick popped up to allegedly do his bit of monster hunting, which may not have been entirely coincidental. Some have suggested that perhaps Slick had a secondary but arguably far more important role in Tibet—namely, to secretly check out the area, forge links to see who was saying what to whom, secure plenty of photographs of the land, and become an influential player and a ferreter and collector of intelligence data at a local level on the growing problems that Tibet was having with China.

It was in the early spring of 1959 that the conflict in the region reached boiling point. On March 10, violent chaos broke out in Lhasa, the capital city, which was under the iron grip of the Chinese Community Party, and had been since 1951. Seen as being a potential threat to the life of the fourteenth Dalai Lama, the fighting quickly prompted secret plans to get him out of the area as fast as possible. And who was at the forefront of this clandestine operation? None other than the CIA's Special Activities Division, which successfully achieved its assignment of getting the Dalai Lama into India, where he created what became known as the Government of Tibet in Exile in Dharamshala. This clearly had the full support of the people of Tibet, as evidenced by the fact that more than 80,000 fellow countrymen eventually followed him.

As for the CIA's Special Activities Division, as the name suggests, this is the one branch of the agency that, perhaps more than any other, takes key and decisive roles in potentially touchy operations relative to intelligence matters. Paramilitary operations are a regular part of its work, as are programs using psychological warfare against the enemy. As we have seen already, psy-war projects were used by U.S. Intelligence in two earlier cryptozoological controversies in the 1950s—the Flatwoods Monster of West Virginia and the Aswang Vampire of the Philippines. A case of first, second, and now, with the Yeti, third time lucky? Quite possibly. Of course, if Tom Slick *was* involved in capers of the spying kind while roaming around Tibet, wouldn't we have some evidence of this—something in his background, the people he mixed with, the places he went? Well, guess what? *We do.*

MONSTER FILES

The name's Slick, Tom Slick

There's very little doubt that Tom Slick did some work for the CIA. He certainly would have been the right person to have on board for such an ingenious project—namely, to do a bit of localized spying under a carefully scripted ruse of looking for a bunch of Yetis. Not only did Slick have a genuine fascination for cryptozoology in general and the Abominable Snowman in particular, but he moved in a lot of powerful circles with numerous significant people—many of whom were linked to the secret worlds of spying, the CIA, official chicanery, and intelligence gathering. One of those, and a good friend to Slick, was Sir Ellice Sassoon, 3rd Baronet, GBE, a resident of Shanghai who spent a great deal of time protecting and advancing Western interests in the Far East and the Orient. Slick's name also appears in the address book of a certain Russian character named George de Mohrenschildt, a petroleum geologist who, upon immigrating to the United States in 1938, was put on J. Edgar Hoover's FBI watch list, following a tipoff from contacts in British Intelligence intimating that he, de Mohrenschildt, was spying for the Germans. On top of that, de Mohrenschildt was in Fort Worth, Texas, in the summer of 1962 and just happened to become pals with none other than one of the most infamous and controversial characters in American history, Lee Harvey Oswald.

De Mohrenschildt believed that Oswald had been a pawn in the shooting of President Kennedy and testified to as much before the Warren Commission. This statement was widely publicized by the New Orleans DA Jim Garrison, who later became a famed investigator of the death of JFK. Notably, James Douglass, the author of *JFK and the Unspeakable*—a book that concludes Kennedy was murdered by elements of the Mafia, CIA and FBI, acting on orders from on high as a direct result of Kennedy's plans to end the Cold War—said of de Mohrenschildt that he "had been Oswald's CIA-approved shepherd in Dallas [who] probably [had] no understanding in advance of the scapegoat role that lay ahead for [Oswald]" (Douglass, 2010).

In addition, de Mohrenschildt was also very chummy with the Bush family. Yes, *that* Bush family. To the extent that while at the Andover, Massachusetts–based Phillips Academy, de Mohrenschildt's nephew, a man named Edward G. Hooker, roomed with none other than President George Herbert Walker Bush. And speaking of Bush Sr., there's a Tom Slick connection there, too, and it's a very significant one. Slick was on the board of directors of an organization that went by the title of Dresser Industries, a multinational outfit based out of Dallas, Texas. It transpires that Henry Neil Mallon, the president of Dresser, gave George H. W. Bush—the director of the CIA and future president—his inroad into the lucrative world of the oil industry. And here's where we see even more evidence of Slick popping up in significant places and with even more significant people.

In the early 1950s, Bush, along with partners Hugh and Bill Liedtke, established Zapata Petroleum, a company that in just a few years was worth millions. In 1954, the president-to-be decided to go it alone and purchased the subsidiary Zapata Off-Shore. By 1958, the company was drilling in Mexico's eastern Gulf. Intriguingly, the islands of the area had been leased to Howard Hughes—himself deeply in bed with the CIA—and plans were made to use them as bases from which to attack Cuba in the early 1960s. And guess who was a very close friend of Hughes back then? Tom Slick. The two even had adjoining premises at the Beverly Hills Hotel!

And so we see Tom Slick mixing with CIA asset Howard Hughes, an outfit (Dresser Industries) that put a U.S. president and CIA director on the road to success, a shadowy and controversy-filled character with links to Lee Harvey Oswald, and a powerful baronet who spent a great deal of time ensuring that the West's influence in the Orient remained strong and vital. And, as if more proof were needed of Slick's ties to officialdom, the family's corporation ran a freight airline service called Slick Airways, whose Douglas DC-4 and DC-6 aircraft and its Lockheed Super Constellations were used in clandestine CIA missions to secretly ferry munitions and agents to areas of the globe where the Agency wished to wield its influence (in other words, pretty much everywhere).

CRYPTOZOOLOGY VS. CRYPTIC-ZOOLOGY

To further support the idea that Tom Slick was an important asset of the CIA, we see that he was not the only one who combined monster-hunting with a bit of daring espionage. There were others in the field of cryptozoology who appeared to be doing exactly the same thing when circumstances demanded it. Sidney Dillon Ripley was just one such example. In the Second World War he was in the employ of the Office of Strategic Services, which was the biggest inspiration behind the creation of the CIA in 1947. From 1964 to 1984, he was also the secretary of the prestigious Smithsonian Institute and a board member of the World Wildlife Fund. Loren Coleman says of Ripley that he was "involved in several cryptozoological episodes, including the search for the Spiny Babbler," a peculiar and elusive species of bird that lives only in Nepal. Concerning Ripley's links to the covert and clandestine world of intelligence, as well as his enthusiasm for seeking out unusual or legendary animals, Coleman has this to say: "There is little doubt he used his searching for multiple objectives" (Coleman, 2006).

Then there is a character named John Chambers, who passed away in 2001. A major force in the world of Hollywood, Chambers was responsible for the groundbreaking facial makeup in the 1968 movie *Planet of the Apes*, for which he deservedly won an Academy Award. Chambers was also openly accused of being the brains behind the so-called Patterson Film, a decidedly controversial piece of footage shot on October 20, 1967, by a man named Roger Patterson, at the Klamath River in California. The film appears to document a large, hairy female Bigfoot on the move. For the record, Chambers denied playing any kind of role whatsoever in the creation of the film. It is, however, most interesting that Chambers was awarded the CIA's highest award for civilians, given his connection to Bigfoot via the Patterson footage, and the fact that he had brought the creatures in *Planet of the Apes* to life. The reason for the award was actually simple and prosaic: He secretly assisted the agency when field agents were required to be disguised using makeup, wigs, and advanced prosthetics.

There were other cryptozoologists who were rumored to have connections to the high echelons of U.S. government. An acclaimed and near-legendary cryptozoologist named Ivan T. Sanderson was the author of many books, including *Abominable Snowmen: Legend Come to Life* and *Green Silence: Travels through the Jungles of the Orient*. Sanderson also happened to have worked for Britain's Naval Intelligence during the Second World War. His specialty: counter-espionage. Then there was Carleton S. Coon, a professor of anthropology at the University of Pennsylvania, a man with a significant interest in the

Abominable Snowman, and, like Ivan T. Sanderson, an asset of the Office of Strategic Services. He was a rumored asset of the CIA, too. And then there's the late anthropologist George Agogino. Not only did he pen the preface to Ivan T. Sanderson's aforementioned *Abominable Snowmen* book, but he was also a consultant to Tom Slick. And Agogino had one more arrow in his quiver: He had been contracted to do work for the CIA in the past.

THE YETI: SOVIET STATEMENTS
AND SECRET FILES

Despite the best attempts by American officialdom to keep everything under wraps, the Soviet government had deep suspicions that the seemingly innocent quests of Tom Slick to seek out the truth about the Yeti were actually far more complex and devious than they appeared to be. Indeed, as evidence of this, on April 27, 1957, none other than the *New York Times* ran an article titled "Soviet Sees Espionage in U.S. Snowman Hunt" that focused on this very issue. Evidently the Soviets had hit on solid intelligence data, since the article in question even referred to the actions of Slick in the region, and Russian concerns about U.S. government agencies using presumed monster hunts as part of a plot involving the "subversion of Communist China" (Ibid.). Most notable of all, the *Times* added, according to the Soviets, the "engineering" of the growing divisions between Nepal and China were prompted by "the missing link in the story of the mysterious scientific expeditions sent to the Himalayas in quest of the 'snowman'" (Ibid.).

While the seething Soviets perceived—certainly correctly— Tom Slick's adventures in Nepal as prime examples of outrageous, undercover espionage, other elements of the U.S. government were far more focused on the reality of the Abominable Snowman itself, rather than the way in which the air of mystery surrounding the beast could be manipulated for intelligence matters. A perfect case in point is documentation declassified by the Department of State dated November 30, 1959, and that originated with the U.S. Embassy at Kathmandu. It tells an undeniably fascinating story. Titled *Regulations Covering Mountain Climbing Expeditions In Nepal—Relating To Yeti*, the document, prepared by Ernest H. Fisk, at the time the counselor of the Embassy, demonstrates a number of criteria for Yeti hunting that had been carefully spelled out in the heart of bureaucracy. First, anyone wishing to search for the monsters had to secure a legal specific permit from the government of Nepal. And second, while it was considered legal to photograph a Yeti, and even capture a living specimen, "it must not be killed or shot at except in an emergency arising out of self defense." More intriguingly, and specifically in relation to matters that might have had bearings upon official secrecy, the Department of State noted two significant matters: (a) that any photographs taken that appeared to show evidence of the creatures had to be surrendered to the Nepalese Government at the earliest opportunity; and (b) any information "throwing light on the actual existence of the creature" was not to be provided to "the Press or Reporters for publicity without the permission of the Government of Nepal" (Ibid.). Fisk noted in the sternest of tones: "These regulations are to be observed" (Ibid.). Mark Murphy, the archivist who stumbled upon the remarkable document more than 50 years after it was prepared, said, "I thought I was seeing things. These documents show that finding the Yeti was a big deal in the 1950s. It goes to show the government was taking this seriously" (Bedard and Fox, 2011).

The three regulations are as follows:

1. Royalty of Rs. 5000/- Indian Currency will have to be paid to His Majesty's Government of Nepal for a permit to carry out an expedition in search of 'Yeti'.

2. In case 'Yeti' is traced it can be photographed or caught alive but it must not be killed or shot at except in an emergency arising out of self defence. All photographs taken of the animal, the creature itself if captured alive or dead, must be surrendered to the Government of Nepal at the earliest time.

3. News and reports throwing light on the actual existence of the creature must be submitted to the Government of Nepal as soon as they are available and must not in any way be given out to the Press or Reporters for publicity without the permission of the Government of Nepal.

FOR THE AMBASSADOR:

Ernest H. Fisk

Ernest H. Fisk
Counselor of Embassy

The U.S. government takes note of the Yeti. © U.S. Department of State, 1959. Source: Department of State, under the terms of the Freedom of Information Act

And there's one final matter of note regarding this document: A copy of it turned up in the archives of none other than the CIA, albeit without any explanation as to why, unfortunately. But, by this stage, it can scarcely be a surprise that matters pertaining to Nepal and the Yeti—and in the very same context and during the same time frame that the land and its people were in a state of violent turbulence—should be held so tightly by the "Men in Black" at the CIA.

Death in the skies and Hollywood interest

And what, you may be wondering, ever became of Tom Slick? Well, therein lies yet another controversial saga: In October of 1962, Slick was flying to Canada in a Beechcraft airplane when it suddenly exploded in mid-air, killing him and showering debris down on the good state of Montana. For some researchers the tragedy was merely one of the many potential hazards that any globe-trotting adventurer might one day unfortunately come up against. For others, however, and taking into consideration the large number of official secrets that Slick may have learned during his time working with the CIA, the old maxim that "dead men tell no tales" is one that should, perhaps, be kept solidly in mind.

But maybe the saga of Tom Slick is not quite over. Back in the 1990s, there were rumors that Nicolas Cage's production company, Saturn Films, was going to make a movie on the life of this extraordinary adventurer, to be titled *Tom Slick: Monster Hunter*, with Cage himself in the starring role. Unfortunately, the project has not yet come to fruition. Maybe one day another Hollywood producer will take up the challenge, and the life of Tom Slick will finally be splashed across the big screen for all to see. And maybe, just maybe, a few secrets regarding both the CIA and the Abominable Snowman will surface, too.

Chapter 10

Secret Agents and a Supersized Snake

Within the history of monster hunting, legends of huge, marauding snakes—far larger than anything that conventional zoology could ever accept as existing today—proliferate. And a great deal of these very same legends originate deep within the jungles of South America, one prime example being Guyana, a sovereign state situated upon the northern coast of South America and bordering a significant portion of the Caribbean Sea. There is one particular part of Guyana where the tales of terror abound—just as the creatures themselves supposedly do. The area in question is a large and impressive mountain range that overlooks a small village called Taushida, home to many a dark and winding cave where the massive beasts are alleged to lurk and feast. During the final weeks of 2007, in what is called the Corona Falls area of mountainous Taushida, a group of explorers from the United Kingdom's Center for Fortean

Zoology's (CFZ) learned that less than a year previously, a huge anaconda had been wreaking havoc and mayhem among the locals. Whatever trepidation they experienced upon hearing this news was perfectly understandable, since the monster was reputed to be more than 40 feet long.

As the CFZ also discovered, another potential domain of a very similar beast was a nearby body of water referred to by locals as Crane Pond. After gaining the trust of the local tribespeople, the team's zoologist, Richard Freeman, was told that sightings of a giant snake dwelling in the vicinity had been whispered about since the late 1950s. Of the several stories he heard, one stood out above all the rest. It, too, concerned events that occurred during the 1950s, a time when there was a great deal of cattle ranching going on around the Crane Pond region. As the tale went, on one particular evening a band of ranchers elected to make their camp on the very edge of Crane Pond, chiefly because it would allow them and their worn-out horses access to a welcome supply of much-needed water without their having to travel in the dark to find it. By the time the night was over, however, one and all probably wished they had chosen a location much farther away. At some point during the early hours of the morning, the band was jolted awake by distinctly loud splashing, and a strange snoring/breathing noise—both of which seemed to indicate the presence of some kind of animal. Panic set in instantly: Men scattered in haphazard fashion, with guns firing wildly into the darkness. The large and shadowy form of something snake-like was briefly seen slithering among the trees in front of them. Not wishing to become the victims of what appeared to be an as-yet-undiscovered species of snake, the group wasted no time in getting themselves and their horses out of there. No-one dared look back to see if the creature was following them; they simply prayed and hoped it wasn't. Not a single member of the group ever returned to Crane Pond, such was the cold grip of dread that had instantly wrapped itself around the hearts of one and all.

Having studied the story carefully, Richard Freeman believes the creature was an anaconda of previously unheard-of proportions. As a noted expert on reptiles, Freeman has a very good reason for believing he has identified the beast of Crane Pond: Anacondas do indeed make a strange sound when they breathe, a sound that has been likened to snoring. While Freeman and his comrades were not lucky enough to uncover proof of any anacondas in excess of 40 feet in length, they did locate a number of anaconda trails during their time spent in Taushida that strongly indicated the presence of snakes measuring around 20 feet long, which is undeniably impressive by itself.

The CFZ group also came across a tale with a degree of conspiracy linked to it. During the late 1990s, Freeman was informed by a local man, an English adventurer had slain in Taushida a mighty anaconda, slightly more than 30 feet long. That same adventurer, Freeman was further informed, was also something of a Tom Slick character. He had a great deal of influential connections at an official level who secretly and illegally shipped the skin of the anaconda to the United Kingdom and then on to his, the hunter's, very own personal collection of cherished animal hides. Given all of this, it appears that Guyana remains a hotbed of super-sized snakes. And it may not be the only place in South America that can make such a bold claim. Bolivia can, too. How do we know this? All thanks to none other than the CIA, of course.

A Bolivian beast and a bunch of spies

At some point in the latter years of the 1950s, CIA personnel working out of the American embassy in Bolivia learned from a nearby cattle rancher that a huge snake—possibly in excess of 30 feet in length—was hiding out in a seldom-explored cave in the area and had devoured almost a dozen of the locals. A true man-eater, then, was holding horrific sway over both the land and its terrified people. Over the course of the next few months, and at various cocktail parties held at the embassy, the story—just like the snake itself, apparently—kept resurfacing and simply would not go away. After yet more violent and tragic deaths occurred, a plan was finally put into action to try to dispatch the menacing beast once and for all. In just the same way that St. George took on a marauding dragon in centuries long past, so the CIA was going to take on a monster-sized snake.

Perhaps relishing the break from listening in on telephone conversations, bugging hotel rooms, and clandestinely following suspicious characters named Ivan or Boris around town, the agents who elected to bag the beast didn't waste any time in getting the plan underway. Once they ascertained the location of the cave, the CIA team carefully and cautiously made their way to its rather imposing entrance. According to one of the team members, a man known only as "Lee," they quickly fired a salvo of tear-gas canisters into its darkened depths and waited with bated breath. They didn't have to wait long, however: The giant snake, moving at breakneck speed, shot out of the cave in an instant and in the direction of the horrified group. Fortunately, they had anticipated this and were well-prepared for almost any eventuality.

Given that the entrance to the cave was not terribly big, the CIA had someone carefully construct for them a large trap

In the late 1950s, CIA agents battled a giant snake in Bolivia. By Joseph Jacobs, 1894.
Source: Wikipedia

comprised of various strong sacks, all strongly lashed together and with tough zippers at either end. Sure enough, as the men had hoped, as the snake raced out of the darkness of the cave to escape the effects of the tear gas, it found itself barreling head-long into the tunnel of sacks, only to meet a dead-end when it slammed into the end zipper. It was a case of quickly getting the other end zipped while the powerful snake thrashed around wildly, likely tossing more than an agent or two into the air like nine-pins, as it tried to make good its escape—which, unfortunately, it did.

Utter pandemonium broke out as the huge monster reared up out of the remains of the shredded sacks and right in front of some of the CIA's finest, who, it seemed, were about to be served up as tasty snacks for the monster. Fortunately for them, but far less so for the snake, that didn't happen. Instead, the afore-mentioned Lee, who had the good foresight to bring along with him a fully loaded gun, let loose with a barrage of bullets into the creature's brain. Since the beast's evil eyes had locked with Lee's only seconds before, when it was in the process of lunging toward him, this was decidedly good timing on his part. It fell to the floor, no doubt with ground-shaking force, utterly dead. When it was finally measured, the animal was reportedly an incredible 33 feet, 3 inches long!

Too good to be true?

David Atlee Phillips was a CIA officer who began his career with the agency in Chile in 1950, and later worked through-out much of Latin America, Cuba, and Mexico. He ultimately became the CIA's chief of operations in the Western hemi-sphere. When he was told of the sensational story—which, it must be said, strains credulity—he exclaimed that Lee simply had to be a liar. Even when he was shown the skin of the snake that Lee had carefully and proudly preserved as prime evidence of the violent confrontation at the cave, Phillips still had seri-ous doubts. He suspected that Lee had acquired the skin under far more prosaic, non-sensational circumstances, and had then jokingly created the amazing tale as an example of titillating, James Bond–like daring. That is, until Phillips had occasion to bring up the matter of Lee and the giant snake of Bolivia with a man named Darwin Mervill Bell, who had spent time in the

1950s working with the Agency for International Development in La Paz, Bolivia, and who later worked for the Peace Corps in Lima, Venezuela, and Peru. When Phillips asked Bell if he knew Lee, Bell replied that he most certainly did, and very well, too. Spurred on by this, Phillips recounted the saga of the snake to Bell, while admitting that he found the whole thing very difficult to believe. "To this day," added Phillips, "[Lee] claims they made a canvas sack with zippers at both ends. Now, did you ever hear anything about that?" (Ranelagh, 1986) Bell's stunning reply, which no doubt immediately and forever put to rest all of Phillips's doubts in the same way that Lee's bullets dispatched the snake itself, was: "Mr. Phillips, I certainly have heard about that. I was the tail zipper man." (Ibid.) In other words, take that!

VALIDATION OF THE LEGENDS

While there still may be those who take the view that stories like the ones provided to Richard Freeman, and that of Lee and the CIA's supersized snake caper of the 1950s, should be accepted only with large portions of accompanying salt—even though the former is a respected expert on reptiles and zoo-keeper, and the latter was a CIA employee with both credentials and influence—there are solid grounds for concluding they should not be dismissed out of hand. We can now say with certainty that massive snakes were indeed once a reality in the jungles and plains of South America.

Discovered barely a decade ago at the Cerrejon coal mine in northern Columbia were the remains of a terrifyingly massive snake that has since become known as *Titanoboa*, a distant relative of both the anaconda and the boa constrictor. It lived almost 60 million years ago, impressively weighed in at around a ton, and grew to the almost unbelievable length of 50 feet. Most amazing of all, fossil evidence suggests it could swallow crocodiles whole. Rather than being the now-extinct animal that zoologists assure us it is, could the *Titanoboa* still be with us? If so, did one of its kind—or, possibly, even the very *last* of its kind—do battle to the death with secret agents of the Central Intelligence Agency back in the 1950s? Perhaps, if the CIA knows more of Lee's story, one day it will choose to share with us the amazing details of it all.

CHAPTER II

AUTOPSYING A MONSTER

Micah Hanks, one of the United States' leading researchers and writers on a wide range of paranormal phenomena, notes that, for decades, there have been rumors suggesting that the world's most famous man-beast, Bigfoot, "might have been acknowledged in some official capacity." He expands: "Folks calling in to late-night radio programs have told odd stories of ape-like creatures being killed, only to be subsequently zipped up in body bags and spirited off by 'Men in Black.'" And he offers a most important question in relation to such matters: "But is there evidence that suggests that they have taken interest in such wild claims, as well?" (Hanks, 2011)

In answer to Hanks's controversial question, the answer may very well be yes. If Bigfoot truly is an animal made of flesh and blood, then logic dictates that the day may finally arrive when a specimen—dead or alive—finally falls into the hands of some lucky someone. But perhaps that day had already come decades ago. And perhaps that "someone" was none other than the U.S. military. It's time to unravel a tale that, if true, suggests Bigfoot is something far weirder than just an uncategorized species of ape, and that elements of the American government are unsettlingly aware of the situation, even if they don't have all the answers regarding its origin, its present mode of existence, or it reasons for lurking—and perhaps even killing—among us.

An alien base

On November 21, 1963, President John F. Kennedy paid a historic visit to Brooks Air Force Base in San Antonio, Texas. He was there to dedicate half a dozen new facilities engaged in cutting-edge research into the mysterious domain of outer space, and particularly so in relation to potential health hazards that might be encountered outside of the Earth's atmosphere by NASA's astronauts. It was one thing to be able to put people into space; it was quite another to ensure they stayed healthy and fit while they were out there. And, as JFK learned, it was the base's 6570th Aerospace Medical Research Laboratories that had the task of overcoming the conditions in outer space, such as deadly radiation and low-gravity environments, that might seriously affect the physical health of NASA's heroes.

Intriguing rumors have long and quietly circulated to the effect that while he was at Brooks, the president was shown something sensational and unearthly: nothing less than one of the alleged alien bodies found at the legendary crash site of what many believe to have been an extraterrestrial spacecraft at Roswell, New Mexico, in the summer of 1947. Granted, it's a highly controversial story, but it's one made all the more controversial and intriguing by several significant known facts. At Brooks, Kennedy met and had a closed-door meeting with a certain Major General Theodore C. Bedwell, Jr. Rather notably, in the period from 1946 to 1947, Bedwell held the position of Deputy Surgeon and Chief, Industrial Medicine, Air Materiel Command at what was then called Wright Field, based in Ohio. As many military old-timers from Roswell maintain, the extraterrestrial corpses found in New Mexico were secretly shipped to a secure location at Wright Field (today known as Wright-Patterson Air Force Base) for study and autopsy. This occurred when Bedwell was on base in a major medical capacity.

Not only that. During the course of his visit to Brooks, President Kennedy had a meeting with a U.S. Air Force colonel named Harold V. Ellingson. He was a brilliant man who was awarded a bachelor of science degree in bacteriology in the mid-1930s. One of the positions that Ellingson held was that of Post Surgeon and Hospital Commander at Fort Detrick, Maryland—the U.S. government's central hub for research into biological warfare and exotic viruses, and also a place where the extraterrestrial corpses have allegedly long been held under secure lock and key. The dedication at Brooks was eventually overshadowed by tragedy, as it was Kennedy's final official act as president before he was shot and killed in Dallas the following day by Lee Harvey Oswald—or the Cubans, or the CIA, or the KGB, or the FBI, or the Mob, or.... The dizzying list of potential candidates is, as most people are aware, practically unending. And now for the controversy concerning Brooks Air Force Base, the aforementioned Major General Theodore C. Bedwell, and the wildest man of the woods himself—Bigfoot.

Sasquatch gets sliced and diced

For the first four years of the 1960s, Bruce Weaver's grand-father, Sam, was employed at Brooks Air Force Base and was a good friend to Bedwell, with whom he shared an interest in avionics and the somewhat-futuristic world of outer-space medicine. But that's barely the tip of the iceberg. According to Bruce Weaver, one of Bedwell's staff had quietly confided in his grandfather that, among the hundreds of classified documents held at Brooks (most of which dealt with how the U.S. military and NASA were both working hard to keep American astro-nauts safe and healthy in outer space) was a top-secret report that truly strained the limits of logic and credulity.

It was a lengthy document—complete with graphic color photographs—of the autopsy of a huge, gorilla-like animal that had been found one morning in 1962 by a security team on the fringes of what is today NASA's John H. Glenn Research Center. Situated at Ohio's Lewis Field, it's an historic locale where the liquid hydrogen rocket engines used in NASA's manned *Apollo* missions to the moon from 1969 to 1972 were developed. As for the strange body, said Sam Weaver, it had reportedly been recovered from within the dense woods that surrounded much of the center.

As the story went, late on the night prior to the astonish-ing find, strange, fast-moving balls of blue light—certainly no bigger than basketballs—were seen by security staff circling the installation at precariously low levels, and flitting in and out of the woods. Whatever they were, they gave every indication of being under some form of intelligent control, but they didn't appear to be hostile. Despite this seeming lack of hostility, Sam Weaver told his grandson that there had been some sort of altercation, that weapons had been discharged by panicky guards at one point, and that the next morning, with the benefit of sunlight, a team scouring the area for evidence of what had been afoot the previous night stumbled across the giant, hairy corpse.

Bruce Weaver stresses that at no point in the files is the beast referred to specifically as Bigfoot. This is not surprising, however. Although the term had already been in use by foresters in California since the late 1950s, in specific reference to wild, hairy men of the woods, in 1962 it was certainly not the sound byte of popular culture that it is today. But, regardless of how the beast was named (or not named) in the files, it seems that a Bigfoot was exactly what the security team had discovered. But, said Sam Weaver, the creature was no gorilla, and it certainly didn't seem to be a kind of ape unknown to science and zoology, either.

The major general's colleague quietly advised Weaver that the animal was enormous: Somewhere around 9 feet tall, very muscular, and weighing in at more than 500 pounds, it possessed 32 teeth and vocal chords similar to those of humans. Strangely, and deeply disturbing to the doctors who were involved in the study of the immense thing, some kind of metallic device that appeared to have been surgically implanted was extracted from the lower part of its left arm. But who had put it there, nobody knew. Theories were tossed around that it was some sort of bug or tracking device, but it all amounted to a great deal of wild speculation and nothing concrete. But the device was there all the same.

That the creature seemed to be somehow connected to the strange balls of flying light seen at the John H. Glenn Research Center the night before its body was found, suggested to some

NASA's Glenn Research Center: A Bigfoot gets autopsied. © NASA, 2000. Source: Wikipedia

of those present at the autopsy a theoretical UFO link. So, with that in mind, the body and the removed device were secretly shipped to Wright-Patterson in Ohio, which was home to many of the Air Force's UFO study programs of the 1940s–1960s as well as its Foreign Technology Division, and—lest we forget— the workplace of Major General Bedwell in 1947. And there the story and its attendant trail go not just cold, but down-right freezing. Nevertheless, Bruce Weaver firmly stands by his grandfather's account of the military's secret autopsy of a monster, as well as the fragments of the story told to him, even if they do stretch credulity to its limits.

Bigfoot on ice—yes, it certainly does sound amazing. But, as will become clearer later, 1962 was apparently not the only year when a Sasquatch reportedly met its maker and was systematically carved up by elements of the U.S. military.

MONSTER FILES

CHAPTER 12

THE STRANGE SAGA OF ACOUSTIC KITTY

In the 1970s hit television series *The Six Million Dollar Man*, military doctors confidently and famously predicted that "we can rebuild him"—a reference to Colonel Steve Austin, a retired U.S. astronaut played by actor Lee Majors, who, after a devastating aviation accident in which he lost both legs, his right arm, and left eye, was carefully and systematically reconstructed using futuristic bionic technology. Austin was quickly transformed into a robotic James Bond endowed with preternatural strength, and the ability to leap tall buildings and run at an impressive 60 miles per hour. While secretly working for the American government's Office of Scientific Intelligence he saved the world from dastardly villains, deadly assassins, Russian spies, and power-crazed military dictators every week in prime time. A decade or so before the bionic man became the hero to kids all across the world, however, there was another half-machine, half–living creature that was destined for the exciting world of espionage and adventure. This one, however, was not the work of Hollywood; it was all too shockingly real. Its name was Acoustic Kitty, a walking, meowing, zombie-like nightmare brought to life by crazed, mad professor–types at the CIA.

Cat-astrophic!

Having recognized for years that dispatching its secret agents to spy on the dastardly Soviets was hazardous and, at times, fatal, by the mid-1960s the CIA was finally able to do something to rectify the danger-fraught situation. The plan was to take the heat off the agency's human agents by turning cats into living, controlled listening-devices, implanted with sophisticated eavesdropping technology that would give them the ability to stealthily keep close tabs on the dreaded commies. This might sound like the stuff of science fiction, but it most assuredly was not. The undeniably ingenious, if a bit crazy idea was taken very seriously by the CIA, and was eagerly embraced by the Agency's top dogs and fat cats. But it was all doomed to end in a surreal and swirling mixture of high farce and tragedy.

Spotty evidence of the existence of the program has now surfaced thanks to Freedom of Information legislation. Heavily redacted CIA documentation of 1967, titled *Views of Trained Cats*, tells at least a part of the catastrophic story. The CIA planned to insert sophisticated microphones and transmitters into the bodies and tails of unfortunate cats and have them prowl around the grounds of the Soviet embassy on Wisconsin Avenue, seeing what snippets of conversation they could pick up and transmit back to headquarters. Not only that:

The program was budgeted at an astonishing $10 million ($4 million more than was spent on poor Steve Austin).

The available documents do not make it clear from where the CIA's Office of Science and Technology (OSI) obtained its first test subject—a rescue center, a veterinarian, or, in a worst-case scenario, some friendly old lady's front yard—but it didn't take long before the Frankenstein-like project began in earnest and someone's poor cat became the government's guinea pig. Rather astonishingly, the first cat survived the surgery, seemed to recover very well from the trauma, and coped admirably with the large chunks of metal, wires, and futuristic gadgetry that were now permanent parts of its remodeled body. But, no one should be surprised to learn that things didn't quite work out as planned. In its typically dry, bureaucratic language, the CIA noted in its files that, with hindsight, the project was not destined to succeed because "the environmental and security factors in using this technique in a real foreign situation force us to conclude that for our [intelligence] purposes, it would not be practical" (*Views on Trained Cats*, 1967). That's putting it mildly and in decidedly tactful terms.

The *real* reason why the operation was shut down so hastily was revealed years later by a certain Victor L. Marchetti, Jr., a now-retired special assistant to the Deputy Director of the CIA. Confirming that a great deal of money had been spent on transforming the clandestine cat into something terrible and inhumane, Marchetti came straight to the point when he said of his colleagues at the agency: "They made a monstrosity." And it was a monstrosity that was incredibly difficult to control. Despite concerted and extensive attempts to train the cat, whenever hunger struck, it would wander off and creep around in search of a tasty bird or a mouse. Clearly, further crazy tinkering was

MEMORANDUM FOR:

SUBJECT: | Views on Trained Cats | for
| Use

    1. Our final examination of trained cats
for | use in the | convinced
us that the program would not lend itself in a practical
sense to our highly specialized needs. Repeated checks
on the state of training and equipment showed us that it
was indeed possible to train

locations; we were not able to visualize |
| use for this technique under conditions that
prevail |
    2. We have satisfied ourselves that it is indeed
possible

| This is in
itself a remarkable scientific achievement. Knowing that
cats can indeed be trained to move short distances |
| we see no reason to believe
that a | cat can not be similarly trained to approach

RELEASED _____ SEP 1983

| Again,
however, the environmental and security factors in using
this technique in a real foreign situation force us to
conclude that, for our | purposes, it would not
be practical.
    3. The work done on this problem over the years
reflects great credit on the personnel who guided it,
particularly | whose energy and imagination
could be models for scientific pioneers.

The CIA makes a monster-cat. © CIA, 1965. Source: CIA, under the terms of the Freedom of Information Act

MONSTER FILES

needed, this time to rewire the cat's brain so that it would be impervious to feelings of hunger. Once the necessary adjustments were made, the day finally came when Acoustic Kitty was driven in the back of an innocuous-looking van to a road near the Soviet Embassy (Edwardes, 2001).

With tension mounting by the minute on the part of those CIA agents who were about to unleash their very own 10-million-dollar cat on the might of the Soviet Union, the doors of the van were slowly and carefully opened, and the transformed creature was placed on the ground and encouraged by its handlers to head across the road toward the grounds of the Soviet Embassy. Bad move. *Very* bad move, actually. The cat had barely gone 15 feet when it was hit and killed instantly by a speeding taxi. Acoustic Kitty was no more.

The agents—probably very relieved that their names are fully deleted from the few available files that the CIA has seen fit to place into the public domain—headed solemnly back to headquarters to break the bad news to their colleagues in the Office of Science and Technology that Acoustic Kitty did not possess the customary feline nine lives. The order to terminate the project was quickly issued, likely to the Agency's embarrassment. From that day on, the cats of the United States were forever safe from both the CIA and conversion into robotic armies of whiskered, purring, transponding monsters.

CHAPTER 13

THE MINNESOTA ICEMAN, THE FBI, AND THE VIETNAM WAR

Midway through the 1960s, a controversial character named Frank Hansen claimed to have in his possession nothing less than a primitive humanoid dating back to the last Ice Age, preserved in a block of ice that was found floating in the cold waters off the coast of Siberia by the amazed crew of a Russian fishing vessel. The primitive-looking specimen, which has since become both infamous and legendary within the arena of monster hunting, is now referred to as the Minnesota Iceman. According to the story, the corpse of the hairy, approximately 6-feet-tall creature had been purchased by an anonymous Californian millionaire, who duly made arrangements for Hansen to exhibit it, which he did in various parts of Canada and the United States, including Illinois, Texas, Oklahoma, and Wisconsin. Rather than being an apelike creature similar to Bigfoot, it appeared to be more along the lines of a primitive human or Neanderthal. Some suggested it was possibly even an example of Cro-Magnon man.

THE QUEST FOR THE TRUTH ABOUT BOZO

Cryptozoologists Ivan T. Sanderson and Bernard Heuvelmans heard amazing rumors of the existence of the beast in early December of 1968 from a man named Terry Cullen, who had seen the Iceman on display a couple of weeks earlier at the Chicago-based annual International Livestock Exposition The pair quickly made for Hansen's compact Minnesota-based trailer later that same month to view the evidence up close and personal. After spending about three days studying the creature in the cramped confines of the trailer they declared it to almost certainly be the genuine article. The primitive man, which they dubbed Bozo, appeared to have a broken arm, and one of its eyes was missing from its socket—possibly the result of it having been violently knocked out. Unfortunately, before a full scientific study could be undertaken, the corpse was returned to its anonymous owner and an elaborate latex copy was substituted in its place. And of course there are claims—which may very well indeed be wholly justified—that there never was a real body, only a carefully created model designed to hoodwink the gullible and wide of eye. Today we're really none the wiser than the monster hunters of all those years ago. But that's not the main thing that concerns us here. Regardless of whether there really was a genuine Minnesota Iceman or just a brilliantly crafted model, the fact is that the story of the creature—manufactured *or* born—attracted interest at an official level.

Conflicting Tales of the Monster's Origin

While the original assertion was that the remains of the Minnesota Iceman were allegedly recovered somewhere off the coast of Siberia, the story expanded into one suggesting the crew of the ship in question thereafter made port somewhere in China, and the body was then quickly seized by elements of the People's Republic of China before being smuggled to Hong Kong and from there on to the United States. A slight variation on this tale suggests it was found stored in a deep-freeze plant in Hong Kong, but had never actually been in the hands of Chinese officials. After the story was afforded growing media publicity, a woman named Helen Westring surfaced and claimed that she herself had killed the Iceman while hunting in Bemidji, Minnesota, in 1966. As for the significant damage to its face, Westring maintained that it was the result of her having expertly shot the Iceman right through the eyeball, killing it instantly. That there have been literally dozens of sightings of Bigfoot in the state of Minnesota certainly made people sit up and take note of Westring's claims. But, just to confuse things even further, Howard Ball, a man who worked on the creation of models for the Walt Disney Corporation, proclaimed that there was a much more down-to-earth explanation for all the controversy: He and his son, Kenneth, had constructed the Iceman. Any kind of proof supporting this claim, however, was not forthcoming. In what was arguably the most intriguing story relevant to the subject at hand, Heuvelmans heard that the beast had been shot and killed by U.S. military forces during the Vietnam War, and then smuggled back to the United States in a body bag courtesy of Uncle Sam's finest. Intimations of an official connection don't end there, however.

Ivan Sanderson, determined to resolve the controversy surrounding the creature/model, took the proactive stance of contacting a primatologist named John Napier, a man with a strong interest in Bigfoot, and who penned a book in 1973 titled *Bigfoot: The Yeti and Sasquatch in Myth and Reality*; he also wielded a good deal of influence with the Smithsonian. Sanderson wondered aloud to Napier if the Smithsonian's staff might be interested in pursuing the matter of the Minnesota Iceman for themselves. Much to Sanderson's satisfaction, it turned out that they were. However, two issues quickly developed. First, the minions at the Smithsonian who were put on the case uncovered evidence—much of it controversial and bordering on hearsay—that Hansen himself had secretly commissioned the construction of the Iceman some years earlier. Or perhaps it was the copy that Hansen commissioned, after the real corpse had been returned to its rightful owner—a man no one could find, identify, or even prove existed outside of Hansen's story. Needless to say, it all got pretty confusing for everyone involved. Second, when word reached the Smithsonian that the creature might have been deliberately killed, its staff became worried that they could have a case of outright murder on their hands if it turned out that the creature was real and some form of primitive human, rather than an unknown animal. So what did the Smithsonian do? It quietly set the Feds on Frank Hansen and hastily distanced itself from the controversy. As evidence of this, in 1970 Hansen himself commented on the interest that his creature provoked in official circles:

"I became extremely nervous when the newspapers in both the U.S. and England pointed out that '...if this creature is real, then there may be a question of how and why it was killed.' The Federal Bureau of Investigation and hordes of lesser law enforcement officials revealed a sudden interest in my specimen" (Hansen, 1970).

In later years, Hansen expanded further on all this. Recalling the heady days of the late 1960s when his specimen was on display, he said that a close friend of his, Sheriff George Ford of Winona County, Minnesota, showed up and informed him that he, Ford, had received an inquiry from a Mr. Brewer—special agent Brewer, actually—at the FBI's office in Rochester, Minnesota, which in turn had received orders from J. Edgar Hoover to find out the true nature of the Iceman. Hansen had no intention of waiting around for the FBI to get on his back: "The whole world was looking for this thing and we were heading down Interstate 94 toward Chicago." The image of J. Edgar Hoover's finest in hot pursuit of Hansen and his Neanderthal specimen provokes justified, amusing imagery of the Keystone Cops meets *Scooby Doo* meets *Harry and the Hendersons*. It would have made a great story if it were true; but such a pursuit never happened. What did happen is that the undeniably mystified Mr. Brewer simply poked around for a while, accepted the explanation that the Minnesota Iceman was either an animal or a hoax—but definitely not some form of human, primitive or otherwise—and went on his way to deal with the daily activities and duties of the FBI. He duly informed J. Edgar Hoover of his conclusions that whatever the Iceman was or was not, it was definitely not something that the Bureau needed to bother itself with, unless it wished to find itself up to its collective neck in a laughable controversy (Simmonds, 1995).

Inevitably, given that he was an astute character who knew how to get the punters to part with good money to see the hairy

A primitive ape-man attracts the attention of the FBI. By Hermann Schaaffhausen, 1888. Source: Wikipedia

enigma, Hansen very soon thereafter created a large and prominent sign that went on display right next to the creature. It read: *The near-man...Investigated by the FBI.* One suspects that J. Edgar Hoover and his band of G-Men, including Mr. Brewer, were hardly impressed or enamored of this development—in which they almost certainly would have played no role had the Smithsonian's staff not worked itself into a panic about a potential murder. But for Frank Hansen, it was a dream come to life, and one which furthered the thick atmosphere of mystery and mythology in the making that surrounded his Minnesota Iceman and its attendant tales of official interest in the story.

The Minnesota Iceman is not the only strange creature with alleged links to the carnage of the Vietnam War, however.

A WINGED WOMAN AND MESMERIZED MARINES

It was a warm summer's evening in 1969, and Earl Morrison, at the time a private serving with the U.S. Marine Corps, was stationed in Vietnam, sitting with two friends atop a bunker situated near Da Nang, a port city on the coast of the South China Sea at the mouth of the Han River. For reasons that

Morrison and his friends could never really fathom, they all looked up almost simultaneously and, to their jaw-dropping astonishment, saw a strange figure crossing the night sky and slowly moving in their direction. "We saw what looked like wings, like a bat's; only it was gigantic compared to what a regular bat would be. After it got close enough so we could see what it was, it looked like a woman, a naked woman" (Worley, 1972). The winged creature, added Morrison, was entirely jet-black in color, but seemed to have a greenish glow about it. As it closed in on the dumbstruck trio and passed over them at a height of barely 6 feet, they could hear the distinct flapping of wings. Too astonished to do anything but remain rooted to the spot in terror, Morrison and his comrades simply stared for three or four minutes until the flying bat-woman finally vanished into the darkness of the Vietnam skies.

THE HAN RIVER HORROR AND A SECRET FILE

In the summer of 2009, building began of a huge bridge designed to span the Han River. It was to be more than 2,200 feet long and 123 feet wide, and boast six lanes to allow for traffic to flow to and from the city of Da Nang and its international airport. The Dragon River Bridge, as it came to be called, was sculpted in the shape of one of the legendary, fire-breathing reptiles of ancient Chinese mythology. The name of the bridge is even more apt, some say, since the waters of the Han River are the domain of a Vietnamese equivalent of the Loch Ness Monster.

Admittedly, sightings of the creature of the river are rare, but they do occur. The fact that they span a number of years makes it much more likely that the beast is real and not a product of myth or imagination. Two important documented cases, rather surprisingly, come not from the files of respected monster-hunters and cryptozoologists, as one might reasonably expect to be the case, but from the now-declassified archives of none other than the U.S. Army. Even weirder still, several eyewitnesses to one of the encounters were from the U.S. Marine Corps, the very branch of the United States Armed Forces that Earl Morrison and his colleagues were with when they encountered the region's resident flying bat-woman back in the summer of 1969.

Titled *"Sea Serpent" Sighting at Han River*, the two-page document in question tells an extraordinary story. On the morning of September 17, 1965, several Marine Corps personnel, along with two personnel from the 311th Air Commando Squadron of the 315th Air Command Group, were flying by helicopter from Da Nang Air Base (today, the Da Nang International Airport), when, while crossing the Han River at low level, they caught sight of something incredible and almost primeval in the waters below. They later told an interviewing officer—who must have been wholly bemused by the strange affair—that it was a huge, bright yellow serpentine creature, easily 80 feet in length. It was swimming downstream at a relatively slow rate of speed very near the surface, which is why they were able to see it so clearly. Couldn't the creature have just been nothing stranger than a large snake, the length of which the team had inadvertently and innocently exaggerated in their state of excitement and amazement? Not according to the eyewitnesses, it couldn't. They claimed that the serpent-like creature possessed four large flippers that, as a result of its striking color, could easily be seen against the background of the dark water. These flippers, along with a powerful thrashing tail, appeared to be pushing the creature along as it swam the length of the Han River. And, as everyone knows, snakes don't have flippers.

Given none of the men thought to take even a solitary, priceless photograph of the beast in the half a minute or so that it was in view before quickly vanishing below the waves, apparently there was some degree of discussion among superior officers to the effect that the whole thing was nothing more than a good-natured hoax. However, each and every one of the men was absolutely adamant that it most certainly was not a hoax, conceding that all thoughts of photographing the creature were eclipsed by the shocking sight of seeing such an immense and strange animal in the first place. After all, how many of us could accurately predict the way in which we might react when confronted by such a shock? It seems likely that far more than a few of us might forget all about the camera in our pocket when faced with an 80-foot-long monster mere feet below us.

While the story was of some interest to the military, particularly since it involved several of their very own highly trained personnel, it obviously had no bearing upon national security, and so the matter was simply and quickly forgotten about, and became nothing more than a curious and little-known aside in the history of the Vietnam War. However, there is one more thing that needs to be mentioned: The author of the document included a very brief footnote stating that institutional memory on the base revealed that an extremely similar creature—even down to the pronounced yellow coloring—had been spotted in the Han River during the late summer of 1962, shortly after U.S. military personnel were assigned to the base to help monitor the activities of the Viet Cong. That we have this additional data in hand is important because it demonstrates that the witnesses in the September 1965 incident were not alone: There were others who had encountered the yellow peril years earlier. Of course, this begs an important question: If there are two reports on this huge river monster, might there be more, still hidden and buried in the old archives of the U.S. Army?

CHAPTER 14

FROM LAKE MONSTERS TO SECRET EXPERIMENTS

For hundreds of years they have been the stuff of dark legends and captivating myths. They are those long-necked, hump-backed, coiled beasts of the watery depths known as lake monsters. For creature seekers everywhere, the likes of the elusive Loch Ness Monster of Scotland, Champ of Vermont's Lake Champlain, and the resident beast of Canada's Okanagan Lake, named Ogopogo, are all too amazingly real. Rather than being the collective results of tall fireside tales, misidentification, hoaxes, folklore, and/or too many potent beverages of the alcoholic kind, these unknown denizens of the deep, which science assures us simply cannot exist, just might be real, after all.

Theories meant to explain their true nature are as wide-ranging and multifaceted as the descriptions of the creatures themselves: massively oversized eels; surviving reptiles from the Triassic, Jurassic, and Cretaceous periods called plesiosaurs;

and giant salamanders are just three of a significant number of potential candidates. There is also the possibility that they (or at least some of them) are the secret creations of governments. No, we are not talking about bizarre, out-of-control biological experiments or futuristic gene-splicing operations run wild, along the disastrous lines of Stalin's ape men of the 1920s or the CIA's Acoustic Kitty of four decades later. Here we're focusing on fabricated "monsters" meant to hide military secrets of the underwater kind.

SHERLOCK, A SINISTER LOCH, AND A MONSTER THAT ISN'T

In the world of on-screen fiction, this exact scenario of using a strange creature to hide a classified government project was achieved in fine and entertaining form in Billy Wilder's 1970 movie *The Private Life of Sherlock Holmes*. Starring Robert Stephens in the title role, it focuses upon the complex tale of a beautiful and mysterious woman who, late one mist-filled night, is hauled out of the freezing depths of the River Thames as she clings precariously to life. She is duly taken to the abode of Holmes and his faithful friend and colleague, Dr. Watson, who eventually learns that her name is Gabrielle Valladon. She hails from Belgium and wants help from London's most famous sleuths to find her husband, an engineer who has mysteriously gone missing. The story then takes an ingeniously bizarre turn, as the intrepid trio end up at none other than Loch Ness, Scotland, where they have a very close and traumatic encounter with Nessie on the cold, moonlit waters of the ancient lake. But Nessie is not what he, she, or it appears to be.

In this film the monster of Loch Ness is a submersible—a very early form of submarine developed, built, and secretly tested in the loch by military scientists of the British government, all under the control of Holmes's brother, Mycroft. In the event that the futuristic craft is accidentally seen by eagle-eyed, and certainly wide-eyed, locals, the device is fitted with a specially crafted plesiosaur-like head and long neck to make people think they have seen a monster rather than a top-secret military prototype. In other words, nothing less than amazing cryptozoological camouflage is at work. Of course Holmes and Watson solve the mystery, and they prevent the technology behind the submarine from falling into the hands of the Germans, for whom Madame Valladon is secretly working and spying, as it turns out. But sometimes it's very hard to know where fiction ends and fact begins—and vice versa! Indeed, *The Private Life of Sherlock Holmes* may have contained far more startling and secret truths than most could scarcely even begin to conceive. It's time for us to now take a trip from a Scottish loch to a lake in Wales.

There's something in the water

For those who speak Welsh, it's known as *Llyn Tegid*. If English is your first language, it's Lake Bala. Regardless of which moniker you prefer, the lake is said to be home to a vile, and reportedly hostile, terror of the deep known locally as Teggie. Lake Bala, located in Gwynedd, has three intriguing characteristics: first, it's the biggest lake of the natural kind in all of Wales; second, it's said to be bottomless; and, third, within its deep waters swims a fish, known as the *Gwyniad*, that dates back to prehistoric times. Granted, the creature is a very small one, but, as monster hunters reasonably ask, if one prehistoric fish lurks in the lake, might there not also be another, perhaps much larger and more savage one (or several)? Certainly this is a fair question, but there's a problem inherent in the logic.

Although people have called the area around Lake Bala their home for centuries, sightings of Teggie—or perhaps more correctly, the Teggies—only began around 1912 or 1913. It scarcely needs mentioning that this provokes an important and controversial question: If monsters really do dwell deep in Lake Bala, then why were they never reported prior to the early years of the 20th century? How could they have suddenly, and literally, surfaced then, but apparently never before? The answers may be found behind the impenetrable veil of military secrecy. There is a longstanding legend in the area—one that, it should be stressed, long pre-dates Billy Wilder's *The Private Life of Sherlock Holmes*—suggesting that in the years leading up to the outbreak of the First World War in 1914, the British Royal Navy embarked on an ambitious and highly classified operation in Lake Bala.

As the odd tale goes, Navy scientists came up with a curious and controversial strategy in the event that war broke out with Germany, as history has tragically shown it did. It centered upon strapping explosive-filled mines to the bodies of trained seals and having them torpedo their way through the waters of the English Channel to their intended targets: German battleships. The thought was that the German crews would be looking for British Royal Navy ships *on* the surface, not seals *below* it, thus significantly increasing the chances of explosive success on the part of the Brits. But, if war did arrive, and the project went from theoretical to real-world status, the government of the day had to first get hold of a bunch of seals, and then find a suitable location in which the animals could be trained in the art of warfare.

Such an ideal site was soon hit upon. It was, of course, Lake Bala. As for where they would obtain the seals, well, that was easy. Deals, all done in the ominous name of national security, were quietly struck with traveling circuses and zoos that were more than happy to give up a few of their animals in exchange for an exceedingly generous amount of the British government's money. But things did not quite go as expected.

While the seals seemed quite happy to be frolicking and playing with their handlers, they were far less enthused with the idea of having dummy-mines attached to them and then signaled to furiously race at the small rowboats the military had strategically placed around the lake that were meant to play the role of German warships. When all is said and done, who can blame them? Perhaps in their own unique and uncanny way they were aware that matters were not destined to go well for them, which is why they became progressively more wary around the people who were preparing them for these "suicide missions." Eventually that wariness gave way to complete disobedience. At that stage, the resigned and weary Royal Navy personnel quickly realized two things: (1) the ambitious plan was clearly not going to work; and (2) in a body of water the size of Lake Bala, there was simply no way to recover the seals and hand them back to the circuses and zoos from which they came. So, the military did just about the easiest thing it could, which was absolutely nothing whatsoever. The seals were left to live out their now-carefree lives and swim, eat, and reproduce to their heart's content.

The Navy actually did do one thing: It began to spread throughout the area rumors to the effect that marauding aquatic monsters were loose in the lake. Granted, this was a calculated and dicey gamble, because it might have had the catastrophic effect of enticing curious throngs of people to descend upon the lake by the hundreds or thousands. Fortunately for the British government, this didn't happen. However, as a result of the creation of this monster myth, the details of the secret experiments—some of which had been picked up on by astute, nosey locals—got buried under a mass of concocted tales of the terrifying Teggie. Moreover, the Germans, always on the lookout for the latest new and novel plans the British had up their sleeves, failed to get wind of the fact that they almost fell prey to "killer" seals. Today, almost 100 years after the tests took place, visitors and residents still talk of occasional brief sightings of large, unknown animals breaking the surface of Lake Bala. Whether Teggie, seals, or both, the jury remains confusingly out—probably much to the satisfaction of the British government, which is likely still somewhat uncomfortable with revealing the truth of how it spent taxpayers' hard-earned money creating this novel "monster" all those years ago.

PADDLER: SERPENT OR SUBMARINE?

Moving ahead in both place and time, we now take a journey across the Atlantic to the United States and the curious saga of Paddler, the resident legendary lake monster of Idaho's huge Lake Pend Oreille, which is more than 40 miles long and 1,000 feet deep. For years, there have been sightings of what gives every appearance of being a large, muscular beast snaking along the deep waters of the lake. For example, on Memorial Day 1985, Julie Green and a group of friends were out on the lake when they encountered an impressively sized V-shaped wake, only 200 yards or so ahead of their boat. Green, showing a great deal of bravery and gumption, gave chase and caught sight of a gunmetal-colored object sailing along, partially obscured by the waves. It was just another day in the saga of Paddler, which dates back to the Second World War. On this matter, Patrick Huyghe, a well respected authority on all things supernatural and mysterious, and someone who has carried out a great deal of research into the saga of Paddler, notes: "The very first mention of the Paddler came straight from the Navy's own Farragut Naval Training Station, established on the southwestern end of Lake Pend Oreille in 1942" (Huyghe, 1997).

Was the U.S. Navy deliberately spreading spurious tales about lake monsters in Lake Pend Oreille during WWII as a way to hide the truth concerning something far more significant and secretive, just as their British naval counterparts had done some 30 years earlier? Quite possibly. In the wake of the terrible attack by Japanese forces on Pearl Harbor in December 1941, the Farragut Naval Training Station was established on the lake, where almost 300,000 American sailors received their basic training. After the war was over, the lake became the regular site for underwater experiments undertaken by the Navy's Acoustic Research Detachment, which still exists in the Farragut State Park on the south side of the lake. Interestingly, as of this writing the ARD confirm that: "*Unique experimental hardware* and *floating platforms* have been developed" there, adding that "future plans include continuation of sonar dome development and submarine silencing and target strength reduction experiments using *large-scaled models* [author's emphasis]" (Naval Acoustic Research Center, 2012).

Keeping this firmly in mind, note the following words from Patrick Huyghe: "In 1949 and 1950, a few years after this secret Navy test site opened, the next two accounts of the lake monster appeared in local newspapers" (Huyghe, 1997).

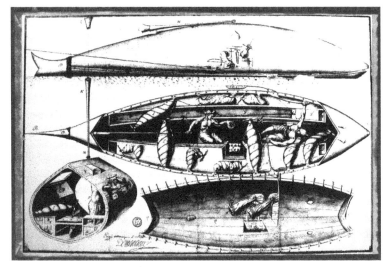

Early submarines that resemble giant fish. By Jean Baptiste Charbert, 1689. Source: Wikipedia

Shadowy serpent or secret sub? No one really knows. But, perhaps the very fact that Julie Green's close encounter of 1985 involved an unidentified, gunmetal gray creature may indicate that, just like the alleged monsters of Lake Bala, Wales, Paddler is not what officialdom would prefer we think it is. This brings us to one other point that we need to resolve.

IT JUST GETS WILDER

The theme of Billy Wilder's *The Private Life of Sherlock Holmes* seems to suggest that the movie legend himself may have had access to more than a few official secrets regarding how monster myths had functioned as brilliant covers for the testing of new and radical underwater technologies. After all, the story that plays out in his movie is strikingly similar to the very real secret programs of submersible subterfuge reportedly carried out in the deep waters of Lake Bala in the 1910s and in Lake Pend Oreille in the United States three decades later. Is there anything to suggest that such a theory has merit, and that Wilder may have had an inroad to a shadowy world filled with official secrecy and the engineering of weird myths? Incredibly, there is.

In 1945, Wilder—who died in 2002—directed the English language version of a documentary titled *Death Mills*, which was produced by the U.S. Department of War's Psychological Warfare Department (PWD). It was a harrowing, but acclaimed, production that graphically revealed the sheer horrific extent of the Nazi holocaust of the Second World War. Notably, the PWD was an office almost identical to (1) the Air Force's psychological warfare group, which appears to have played the central role in the saga of the Flatwoods Monster in 1952; and (2) the agency that orchestrated the legend of the Filipino Aswang vampire in the same era. The Pentagon describes psychological warfare as "[t]he planned use of propaganda and other psychological actions having the primary purpose of influencing the opinions, emotions, attitudes, and behavior of hostile foreign groups in such a way as to support the achievement of national objectives" (Tims, 1975).

A convincing argument can be made that "influencing the opinions, emotions, attitudes, and behavior" of people who may have encountered in either of these lakes, something that the military might have preferred they hadn't seen, would have been prime candidates for the very group of people that Billy Wilder was working alongside in 1945. That the man himself had to sign a number of secrecy oaths with the PWD, some of which were focused on plans for a follow-up movie, at the time of filming *Death Mills* (a shelved project documenting terrible biological experiments undertaken on people during the Second World War by Japan's notorious Unit 731 outfit) is a solid indicator that Wilder moved easily and effortlessly in notable, classified circles. Just perhaps, those same classified circles exposed him to the strange saga of the kind of monstrous manipulation that went on to become the key ingredient of his cryptozoological masterpiece, *The Private Life of Sherlock Holmes* (Ibid.).

And there's one final fact that suggests Billy Wilder knew a great deal indeed about the ways and means by which officialdom was using tales of monsters to hide matters of a very different—and very secretive—nature. At one point in *The Private Life of Sherlock Holmes*, the famous detective notes to his brother, Mycroft, that perhaps Her Majesty's government was using expeditions to the Himalayas to seek out the Yeti as convenient cover stories to allow its agents to engage in a bit of local espionage. In reference to the Diogenes Club—a club cofounded by Mycroft that boasted numerous powerful and influential people in its ranks—Holmes notes: "When there is trouble along the Indian frontier, some of your fellow members pop up in the Himalayas, allegedly looking for the Abominable Snowman" (*The Private Life of Sherlock Holmes*, 2013). Quite clearly, this is an undeniable nod in the direction of the saga of Tom Slick and the theories regarding his so-called monster-hunting. There is little doubt that Billy Wilder knew at least some of the truth of how governments were manipulating monster legends, and that they had been doing so for years. Clearly he was not against revealing a few snippets of those same secrets to which he had been exposed in good-humored fashion on the big screen. You could almost say they were secrets that he hid in plain sight.

CHAPTER 15

SASQUATCH, UFOS, AND THE U.S. AIR FORCE

Stan Gordon is a well-known and long-term researcher, writer, and overall authority on many things paranormal, including UFOs and Bigfoot—sometimes at the very same time. Indeed, between 1972 and 1974, Gordon spent countless hours doggedly investigating a deeply weird wave of activity in his home state of Pennsylvania. It appeared that Sasquatch and unusual aerial lights were repeatedly being encountered simultaneously and in the same location. But that's not all: When Bigfoot and these anomalous phenomena in the skies surfaced, so did certain elements of both the U.S. government and the Air Force.

The events of 1972 to 1974 amounted to nothing less than a swirling, cosmic cauldron filled with shadowy and ominous woods, glowing-eyed and giant-sized beast-men prowling the countryside by night, strange lights in the heavens above, UFO landings, and neighborhoods and families gripped by cold, stark terror. It's thanks to Stan Gordon's research, as well as his in-depth files prepared when the dark drama was at its very height, that we're now able to fully appreciate the curious chaos and calamity that collectively hit the unsuspecting people of Pennsylvania all those years ago. A number of researchers recognize that as much as it would be preferable to place Bigfoot in the category of a real, flesh-and-blood animal, there is a significant and undeniable body of data and testimony that point in a completely different direction. Stan Gordon just happens to be one of those researchers. Small wonder, because the Pennsylvania Bigfoot of the early 1970s that Gordon personally made it his business to find was seemingly impervious to bullets, mysteriously appeared whenever and wherever there were UFOs, and had a disturbing and baffling ability to vanish in the blink of an eye—literally.

THE GOVERNMENT PAYS A VISIT

In September 1973, when the sightings of hairy humanoids and unidentified aerial phenomena were being reported in Pennsylvania, Stan Gordon received a telephone call from a man who seemed deeply interested in his research. The caller tactfully suggested that if Gordon came across any physical evidence suggesting that Bigfoot really did exist, officialdom would dearly like to know about it. If he came across anything of such a nature, Gordon was told he should quickly contact the Bureau of Sports Fisheries and Wildlife, which was created as a part of the U.S. Fish and Wildlife Service in the Department of the Interior in 1956. Since the agency is at the forefront of enforcing federal wildlife laws and protecting endangered species, the request made to Gordon makes a great deal of sense. But it didn't end there.

One month later, on October 2, 1973, Gordon received a visit from two employees of the office of Pennsylvanian Congressman John H. Dent. Stressing that both men were courteous and nonthreatening, Gordon added they seemed open-minded and very curious about the reports of Bigfoot/UFO activity that had descended upon rural Pennsylvania. They seemed very interested, indeed, when he informed them of the phone call of the previous month in relation to Bigfoot and the Bureau of Sports Fisheries and Wildlife. As Gordon recalls: "We kept in touch as the wave of sightings continued." Then, in the latter part of 1973, there came what was undeniably the strangest development of them all (Gordon, 2010).

STRANGE VISITORS

Included in the people with whom Stan Gordon had been liaising during this time period was a man (given the pseudonym of "Steve Palmer") who had been a witness to both UFO and Bigfoot activity at the same time, on the night of October 25, 1973, in Fayette County. It was at approximately 9:00 p.m. when Palmer had a close encounter on farmland with a huge, luminous object and two very tall, dark figures with extremely long arms and eyes that glowed an eerie bright green. As the beasts moved forward across the fields of the farm in Palmer's direction, he opened fire with his rifle. The creatures—apparently utterly unharmed by the bullets—simply turned on their tails and vanished back into the cover of darkness. Likewise, with regard to the UFO itself, it was a case of here one second and gone the next. Perhaps even stranger than that was what happened around 1:00 a.m., when Stan Gordon visited Palmer, after getting a phone call from a state trooper who had been out to the site, in order to get the full details of what had occurred only a few hours previously.

Gordon and several colleagues, including George Lutz, a former Air Force pilot, a photographer named Fred Pitt, a physics teacher by the name of David Smith, and Dennis Smeltzer, a sociology major, headed out to meet with Palmer at the site of the extraordinary encounter when something amazingly bizarre happened. While they were walking around the field where the events of several hours earlier had taken place, Palmer was suddenly transported into some nightmarish, altered state of mind and started breathing very heavily and deeply. He started to growl in a decidedly savage, animalistic fashion—almost as though he were demonically possessed—and then violently threw both his own father and Lutz to the ground.

Things then went from bad to even worse: Smeltzer began to feel light-headed, Pitt had trouble breathing, Palmer keeled over face-first, and the whole area became saturated with an odor akin to that of rotten eggs; sulfur, or perhaps devilish brimstone might be a far more accurate and apt description. Clearly it was time for them to get the hell out of the field, which they did. After he recovered from the shock, Palmer told the group that while in his bizarre, altered state he encountered a black-robed figure (carrying a sickle, no less) that warned him that if humankind did not change its ways, the world would soon come to a terrible end. It was, to put it concisely, quite a night. But it was not the end of things.

Around two weeks later, Palmer got a knock at the door of his home. Opening it, he was confronted by two men, one dressed in a regular suit and the other in the easily recognizable uniform of an Air Force officer. They were there to talk about Palmer's experience in the field on that terrifying night. They confided in him that he should not consider himself crazy, for one very good reason: The Air Force secretly knew that Bigfoot and UFOs were all too real! This became graphically and memorably apparent when the man in uniform pulled out of his briefcase a number of photographs, some of which showed strange objects in the skies: UFOs. But what really stood out were the photos displaying Goliath-sized, hair-covered man-beasts that, as Palmer was informed, had been taken around various parts of the United States. One picture, as Palmer recalls, was particularly memorable; it came from somewhere in Georgia and appeared to have captured a Bigfoot carrying a pig under one of its arms.

The mysterious duo—who clearly evoked the classic "Men in Black" archetype, even if their clothing did not—wanted to know two things: (1) did any of the creatures Palmer saw on the night in question resemble those shown in the photographs; and (2) would he consent to being hypnotized? Well, yes the creatures *were* similar to those Palmer encountered, and yes, he *would* agree to being hypnotized, if only to ensure that the Air Force had all the information on what had occurred. After the session was over and the pair was seemingly satisfied with the data and results obtained, they thanked Palmer and went on their way, promising to get back in touch. They never did. The whole unsettling affair remains a mystery to this very day.

Evidence of the Air Force taking a secret interest in Bigfoot in the 1970s is not limited to the discoveries of Stan Gordon. In the early 1990s, British UFO researcher and authority Timothy Good focused much of his time investigating stories of UFO encounters, disturbing mutilations of farm animals, and Bigfoot sightings, all of which occurred on a Colorado ranch back in the mid-1970s. One of the people involved, a rancher named Jim, made inquiries with an officer from a nearby Air Force installation about what was afoot and was told that "the base had had its share of troublesome UFO incidents, and that directives existed on how to deal with them. The officer also asked Jim if he had experienced any trouble with Bigfoot. Apparently, the Air Force had directives on these elusive creatures, too" (Good, 1991).

Similarly, Jack Lapseritis, a Bigfoot researcher who believes the creatures to be highly advanced psychic entities with direct links to the UFO controversy, has stated the following: "After giving a lecture in Los Angeles in 1994, a well-educated man cautiously approached me. He began by saying: 'Are you aware that everything you stated in your lecture about a Bigfoot/UFO connection is true and that the CIA knows all about it?'" (Lapseritis, 2005) The man further informed Lapseritis that he had a friend, a psychic, who had been secretly contracted by the CIA to try and locate a Bigfoot for them. The operation was reportedly a success: The beast's lair was found, and, after being hit by one of the Jeeps involved in the operation, it was captured and deemed to have otherworldly origins. To be sure, it's a brief story, lacking in full description and data regarding how the military knew the creature to be of an unearthly nature, but it's one that does dovetail with what we have already seen.

Just to add a bit more confusion into the mix, there is the story of the late Gabe Valdez, who in 2009 revealed he had uncovered information that led him to believe that many New Mexico–based Bigfoot sightings were actually the covert work of an arm of the U.S. government that possessed the ability to create holographic imagery of the hairy man-beasts. The purpose: to scare people and deter them from getting too close to some of its secret underground bunker installations. Before you simply dismiss Valdez's assertions, it's worth noting that he was a highly respected police officer in New Mexico for many

Nick Redfern with Bigfoot researcher and police officer Gabe Valdez. © Nick Redfern, 2009.

years, and was extensively consulted by the FBI in the late 1970s when the northern part of the state was hit by a particularly widespread and large number of what have infamously become known as cattle mutilations.

OPENING THE DIMENSIONAL DOORWAYS

Why might there be a connection between UFOs and Bigfoot? What could possibly account for the mystifying, sudden, and literal vanishings of hairy beasts all across Pennsylvania from 1972 to 1974? For answers we need to turn to the studies of an acclaimed Irish investigator of paranormal phenomena named Ronan Coghlan. He sat down with me and explained his theory in 2011:

It's now becoming acceptable in physics to say there are alternative universes. The main pioneer of this is Professor Michio Kaku, of the City College of New York. He has suggested that not only are there alternate universes, but when ours is about to go out in a couple of billion years, we might have the science to migrate to a more congenial one that isn't going to go out. I think he expects science to keep improving for countless millennia, which is very optimistic of him, but whatever one thinks about that, the idea of alternative universes is now gaining an acceptance among physicists, and he's the name to cite in this area (Redfern 2011).

This poses far more questions than it answers, however, as Coghlan himself openly acknowledges:

Now, how do you get into, or out of, alternative universes? Well, the answer is quite simple: You have heard of wormholes, I'm sure? No one has ever seen a wormhole, I hasten to add. They are hypothetical, but mainstream physicists say they could be there, and there's one particular type called the Lorentzian Traversable Wormhole. Physicists admit there is a possibility that this exists, and it would be like a short-cut, from one universe to another. Thus, for example, it's rather like a portal: Something from the other universe would come through it. Or, something from another planet could come through it (Ibid.).

Turning his attention toward the links between wormholes and bizarre beasts, Coghlan had this to say:

If there are any of these wormholes on Earth, it would be quite easy for anything to come through, and it's quite possible any number of anomalous creatures could find their way through from time to time. I have the distinct suspicion we are dealing with window-areas that either contact some other planet, or they contact another universe. My money is on the other universe, rather than the other planet, to be honest with you. Either a short-cut through time, or a short-cut through space, is recognized as possible these days. This is kind of cutting-edge physics, as it were.... Now, the other one isn't cutting-edge physics at all. It's my own little theory. I think, looking at a great many legends, folk-tales, and things of that nature, it is possible to vibrate at different rates. And if you vibrate at a different rate, you are not seen. You are not tangible. And then, when your vibration changes, you are seen, and you are tangible; maybe that this has something to do with Bigfoot appearing and disappearing in a strange fashion (Ibid.).

On the final question of how UFOs come into play in this particular scenario, Coghlan equivocates:

Quite a large number of Bigfoot-type creatures have been seen in the vicinity of UFOs. I'm not saying there's necessarily a connection between the two, but they do—quite often—turn up in the same areas. Now, if UFOs travel by wormholes, and if Bigfoot does the same, that might allow for a connection between the two. They might not be mutually exclusive (Ibid.).

The theories of Ronan Coghlan are not just thought-provoking; they also offer some meaningful answers to a number of the biggest and most problematic issues about Bigfoot that Stan Gordon has raised, such as the lack of a living or dead specimen, the meager if not nonexistent evidence of Bigfoot's eating habits, and its uncanny ability to always avoid capture—not to mention the fact that the beast appears to be well-nigh bullet-proof, too.

Coghlan's ideas may also go some way toward explaining the secret interest in Bigfoot exhibited by certain elements of the U.S. Air Force. Perhaps it is not so much the creature itself that the military is fascinated with; rather, it may be that the Air Force dearly wishes to understand the true nature of wormholes, and how to access them and travel within them for strategic advantage and military gain over potential foreign aggressors. If so, and if there is even the remotest suspicion that Bigfoot is somehow able to hop between dimensions, the idea that the military has taken an interest in the creature and its actions makes a great deal of sense. Although this may sound controversial in the extreme, it not at all an impossible scenario. Though most people probably think that being able to leap across space and time is solely the stuff of science fiction, for years the U.S. Air Force has secretly taken an interest in this strange but potentially world-changing subject. For firm evidence of this, we have to turn our attention to something known as the Teleportation Physics Study.

Beam me up, Bigfoot

The Air Force Research Laboratory, Air Force Materiel Command, quietly contracted this study to Eric W. Davis of a Las Vegas–based outfit called Warp Drive Metrics. It was in August of 2004 that military officials finally made Davis's report readily available to the public and media. Interestingly, the Davis report noted that "anomalous teleportation has been scientifically investigated and separately documented by the Department of Defense" (Davis, 2004). Keep in mind the reasons why the U.S. government and Air Force might want to understand the true nature of a dimension-hopping Bigfoot when Davis notes that teleportation would "represent a phenomenon that could offer potential high-payoff military, intelligence and commercial applications. This phenomenon could generate a dramatic revolution in technology, which would result from a dramatic paradigm shift in science. Anomalies are the key to all paradigm shifts" (Ibid.). Perhaps most notable of all—with respect to the data recounted in this chapter, at least—Davis's report devotes a significant amount of content to how "traversable wormholes" may satisfy the search for a solution "compatible with the concept of teleportation."

CHAPTER 16

BACK IN THE U.S.S.R.

While the strange saga of Joseph Stalin's ape men is both fascinating and disturbing, it does not represent the entirety of Soviet research into the weirder aspects of animal life, as we shall now see. For decades, the U.S. Defense Intelligence Agency (DIA) has delved deeply into the mysterious worlds of psychic phenomena, extrasensory perception, and the paranormal powers of the human brain. The DIA has also focused on the mind skills of other living creatures besides humans. Dogs have been a particular favorite of the DIA, particularly the many and varied "psychic hounds" of the former Soviet Union.

The U.S. government initiated this strange, canine caper in 1975 in order to try and determine if studying the presumed supernatural skills of dogs in the USSR might provide the United States with some sort of military or intelligence-related advantage over the Soviets. This endeavor was then very much akin to a new and revamped look at the groundbreaking research that Joseph Rhine was secretly hired to undertake for the U.S. Army back in the early 1950s, in relation to using animal ESP to locate land mines on battlefields. Rhine's legendary German Shepherds, Tessie and Binnie, were long gone by 1975, but in the heart of Soviet Russia, their equivalents, Tesski and Binnski, were just waiting in the wings.

COLD WAR CANINES

In the 1975 report in question, titled "Telepathy in Animals," the unnamed DIA author states as follows:

> Soviet research on telepathy in animals in the 1920s and 1930s was devoted largely to proving that telepathy between man and animals did indeed exist. A good example of the early Soviet approach was research conducted by V.M. Bekhterev of Leningrad University. In collaboration with a circus performer, [he] reported that trained dogs successfully solved arithmetic problems and identified or retrieved objects solely on the basis of their trainer's mental suggestion (Defense Intelligence Agency, 1975).

The DIA was careful to note, however, that the test results were, at least in some cases, apparently being influenced by whether or not the circus performer was present. In other words, when the handlers were not around, the dogs did not do quite as well in their tasks as when they were present. This did not lead the DIA to think that outright fakery was at work, however; rather, it simply inspired those working on the project to dig deeper and figure out why this was the case. The DIA learned from its careful and secret study of Soviet research in this particular field that Bekheterev's initial goal had been to

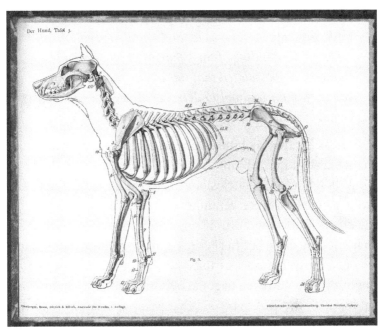

Soviet secrets of the canine kind. By Hermann Dittrich, 1889. Source: Wikipedia

prove, based upon his personal suspicions, that ESP between human and dog resulted from "some form of electromagnetic radiation," or EMR. This theory continued to be pursued by Soviet scientists for many years, as the DIA noted in its report: "The EMR theory of information transfer is still unresolved by the Soviets, but is still the major basis underlying much of their research" (Ibid.).

Even 30 years after Bekheterev was hard at work trying to crack the secrets of how successful mind-to-mind contact could be achieved between humans and dogs, Soviet research was still pushing ahead at full throttle. That same research was also delving into virtually uncharted and even more mysterious waters, as the DIA's findings made amply clear:

In 1962 B.S. Kazhinskiy advanced the theory that animals are capable of visual and aural perception and reflex understanding of the behavior of other animals or humans. He postulated that this ability resulted from the capacity of one animal to detect analyze, and synthesize signal-stimuli given off by another animal (Ibid.).

Or, as Kazhinskiy himself preferred to describe it, a "bioradiational sight ray" (Ibid.).

If Kazhinskiy's conclusions concerning both visual and aural perception were genuine, suggested the authors of the DIA report, then the startling possibility could not be ruled out that not only dogs, but the *entire* animal kingdom of our planet possessed psychic powers that were far more advanced than anything we could even begin to fathom. Bringing matters right up to 1975, the DIA recorded that a Soviet scientist, one A.S. Presman, had concluded that so-called "electromagnetic signaling" was universal between animals, but not, unfortunately, among the people, who "may have lost the capability for such communication as a result of evolution and the development of verbal and artificial communication channels" (Ibid.). The DIA concluded that, by the mid-1970s, Russian studies of ESP in animals were the most advanced of their kind up until that point. Noting that the terms "ESP" and "telepathy" were rarely used by Soviet scientists at that time, the DIA reported that the early research of the 1920s and 1930s had been replaced by "sophisticated research protocols which study complex interactions between man, animals and plants" (Ibid.).

With all of this in mind, it is worth considering one final point. As of this writing the Defense Intelligence Agency's report was written nearly 40 years ago and it represented the sum total of what was known about such matters at that time. This surely begs an important question that could have a major bearing upon national security in this, the second decade of the 21st century: What kind of amazing, paranormal research could the Russians be working on today that we don't know about? Only time will tell.

CHAPTER 17

ARE WE READY FOR BIGFOOT?

On December 21, 1977, the U.S. government's Department of the Interior, Fish and Wildlife Service (DoI) published a controversial and thought-provoking document titled *Are We Ready for "Bigfoot" or the Loch Ness Monster?* The opening of the document was eye-catching and raised some important questions:

> *What if they really did find the Loch Ness monster or the legendary Bigfoot of the Pacific Northwest? Most scientists doubt that these creatures exist, but thoughts of the discovery of a new species that might be the closest living relative to man, or the possibility of finding a leftover dinosaur, excite the imagination of scientist and nonscientist [sic] alike. It also poses another question: Would such a creature be subjected to the same kind of exploitation as the giant movie ape, King Kong? (Department of the Interior, 1977)*

The DoI noted that most scientists at the time accepted that our world was likely home to a number of types of bird and mammals that were still unknown to the scions of conventional zoology, chiefly due to their scarcity in numbers and the remoteness of their respective locations. The agency expanded on this idea by noting that in some parts of the world, at least, up until the latter part of the 19th century, both giant pandas and gorillas were thought to exist only in folktales and myths. Today, of course, we know differently. Clearly having done its homework, the DoI added that the Komodo dragon—an extremely dangerous lizard indigenous to the islands of Indonesia that can grow to a length of around 10 feet—remained undiscovered until the early part of the 20th century. It also brought up the astonishing fact that, in 1935, a deep-water prehistoric fish known as a *coelacanth*, which was presumed to be extinct for 65 million years, was captured very much alive off the coast of Madagascar. Bringing matters up to date for that time, DoI staff noted that "[j]ust last year [in 1976] a Navy torpedo recovery vessel dropped a sea anchor into 500 feet of water off Hawaii. But instead of a torpedo, it hauled up a 15-foot representative of a new species of shark. The dead shark, named megamouth after its bathtub-shaped lower jaw, had an enormous, short-snouted head and 484 vestigial teeth" (Ibid.).

How to handle monsters

So, with amazing discoveries of large unknown animals and fish occurring right up until 1976, what about the monsters of *our* time? What did the Department of the Interior think of the idea that they might really be out there? Let's see what officialdom had to say. Admittedly, the DoI stressed there was an unfortunate and troubling lack of physical specimens or remains of monsters, that none could be found in zoos anywhere, and that the whole situation was made even more problematic and controversial by such matters as mistaken identity and hoaxes. But if such coveted hard evidence finally fell into our eager hands one day, it would be a discovery of a lifetime, the author of the report noted. Of that, there's no doubt whatsoever. In the DoI's very own words:

> finding a Loch Ness monster or Bigfoot is still a possibility, and the discovery would be one of the most important in modern history. As items of scientific and public interest they would surely command more attention than the moon rocks. Millions of curiosity seekers and thousands of zoologists and anthropologists throughout the world would be eager to 'get at' the creatures to examine, protect, capture, or just look at them (Ibid.).

This raised an important question for the DoI, and equally so for the subject matter of the very book you are reading right now: "What would the United States Government do?" (Ibid.)

Bigfoot confirmed

Keith Schreiner, who was the associate director of the U.S. Fish and Wildlife Service at the time, said forthrightly and vocally that he seriously doubted that any action would ever need to be taken, since "I don't believe there are any of the things around to be discovered in the first place" (Ibid.). Fair enough, but this statement did not deter the DoI from speculating on the potential outcome if, for example, Bigfoot were proven to exist beyond a shadow of doubt. They brainstormed potential scenarios regarding how the American populace might react to

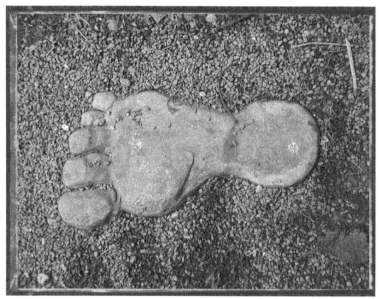

The U.S. government ponders the existence of Sasquatch. © Nick Redfern, 2009.

an official admission that the forests of the United States were the homes of monsters: Would there be terror? Unbridled mass hysteria? Panic and looting? Then there was the public safety angle to consider—namely, people roaming the woods and forests of North America, armed to the teeth and looking to bag a Bigfoot of their very own. Mistaking someone for a Bigfoot on a dark and stormy night in the forests of the Pacific Northwest and then blowing the victim's head clean off would not have had a positive outcome for either hunter or victim, to say the least. Bigfoot, though, would have been mightily lucky to have made its escape at the expense of an unfortunate human casualty. For the DoI, it was important and potentially catastrophic issues such as these that needed to be addressed, just in case Bigfoot were ever elevated—possibly even overnight—from legend to stark reality.

Interestingly, the DoI mentioned the likelihood that confirmation of Bigfoot's existence would likely bring the full power of the U.S. government into the picture immediately:

> *Some officials doubt whether any State or Federal action short of calling out the National Guard could keep order in the area within the first few hours or days of the creature's discovery. This could be essential until a team of scientists could do the necessary things to ensure the creature's survival* (Ibid.).

And how, precisely, might Bigfoot's survival be guaranteed in the wake of an announcement that the creature was all too real? For the DoI, the answer lay in the pages of the Endangered Species Act, which "pledges the United States to conserve species of plants and animals facing extinction. This broad, complex law protects endangered species from killing, harassment, and other forms of exploitation" (Ibid.). It goes without saying this would not have been a simple process, either back in 1977 or today, when it came to a hair-covered man-beast of the forest. According to the DoI, several key and critical issues would immediately come into play, the first of which would undoubtedly be the classification of and name assigned to the beast. Moreover, the report noted, if Bigfoot was shown to be specifically a "U.S. species," then "the Governor of the State where it was found would be contacted, as would the officials of foreign governments if it were found outside the United States. Only after much information was collected could the Service make a formal determination as to whether the species should be afforded endangered or threatened status" (Ibid.).

The DoI touched on a brief bit of history and background of the Bigfoot, noting that the creature was generally described as being around 8 feet tall, weighing in at close to 1,000 pounds, and primarily making its home in the sprawling, mighty forests of the Northwest. The DoI also commented on the "pendulous pair of breasts" and "tall, long-legged, gorilla-like" appearance of one of the animals that had been spotted. It also described how the local government of Skamania County in Washington State was fully prepared to impose a fine of $10,000 and a five-year jail term on anyone who was found guilty of killing a Bigfoot—this, given the large number of people with high-powered rifles intent on finding and slaughtering such an animal. Adding even more enlightening data on the connection between Bigfoot and the U.S. government, the DoI added that the Army Corps of Engineers had listed Bigfoot as "one of the native species in its Environmental Atlas for Washington" (Ibid.), and revealed that earlier in 1977, the Florida and Oregon legislatures were both considering passing bills that would offer protection to the Bigfoot, whatever they might actually be. Keith Schreiner, despite being a confirmed skeptic of Bigfoot, was willing to add the following to that:

> Under normal situations, we must know a great deal about a species before we list it. How big is the population? Does it occur anywhere else? Is the population in danger of decline? Is its habitat secure? Is the species being exploited? What is its reproductive rate? Obviously, if a Bigfoot really were found we could use emergency provisions of the Act to protect it immediately. But for the record, I seriously doubt whether such a creature really does exist (Ibid.).

A few final few words from the DoI made it clear that it would be free to turn its careful scrutiny toward any other bizarre beasts that might be found in the future:

No requests have so far been received for the protection of the reputed foul-smelling Noxie monster, a 7-foot denizen of Oklahoma, or the skunk ape of the Everglades, or the infamous Mothman in West Virginia. But in time, they, too, might come. And when they do, they'll be treated accordingly (Ibid.).

If the account described in Chapter 11, concerning the alleged recovery and autopsy of a Bigfoot body in Ohio in 1962, is true, quite clearly those elements of the U.S. military that reportedly handled the incredible event must have thought that sharing the data with the likes of the Department of the Interior was a definitive no-go. This is not at all an unlikely scenario, however. Within the domain of government secrecy, both the need to know and the need *not* to know are daily ways of working life. Given that, as interested as the DoI clearly was in the Bigfoot phenomenon in 1977, it appears not to have been sitting on any kind of monstrous smoking gun, so we are left to conclude that whatever the military possesses stays strictly with them. Seemingly, that applies to secret knowledge of the existence of Bigfoot, as well.

CHAPTER 18

A MOUNTAIN OF SECRETS

When Mount St. Helens erupted in May 1980, it was a terrible, life-changing disaster for all of the people who called the area home. For some, tragically, it was not just life-changing: It was life-claiming. It may have been a similarly terrible tragedy for Bigfoot, too. For years, reports, tales, and rumors have circulated wherever cryptozoologists hang out, of large, lumbering, hairy giants roaming the ancient mountain. Indeed, such stories date as far back as the time of the pre-Columbian Native Americans. But, as we have already seen on several occasions, where there is talk of Bigfoot, there is very often talk of conspiracy, too. This also holds true for the events that occurred at Mount St. Helens in Washington State more than 30 years ago. A significant number of people from all walks of life—members of the public, military personnel, forestry workers—have told eerily similar tales of Army helicopters flown into the area in the immediate wake of the disaster, and that allegedly secretly airlifted out of the area the bodies of massive, ape-like animals that were killed in the eruption. Their destination: unfortunately unknown. In this affair, are we looking at a modern-day myth, sensationalist hearsay, or stark reality? There's only one way to be sure. Let's take a trip back in time to the day when all hell broke loose both on the ground and in the skies of Washington State.

The mountain erupts

For about two months prior to the cataclysmic events of May 18, 1980, it was clear that something ominous was looming in the area. Earthquakes, from mild to more intense, and reports of large amounts of scalding hot steam escaping from the 8,365-foot-high mountain, became all too disturbingly commonplace. Personnel from the United States Geological Survey (USGS), which quickly and astutely realized that matters were likely to end in carnage and tragedy, wasted no time in closing the mountain to hikers, hunters, the public—anyone who had no official reason for being there when danger threatened. The USGS also urged in the strongest terms possible that those living in the area should evacuate immediately—as in *yesterday*. Some heeded the warning but, sadly, others did not—to their great and fatal cost, unfortunately.

Around 8:30 a.m. on May 18, the rumblings and murmurings that had been issuing forth from the old and mighty mountain for eight weeks or so finally reached their boiling point: a catastrophic earthquake caused the entire north face of Mount St. Helens to literally disappear, crumbling away and falling at speeds in excess of 150 miles per hour. It was followed by an eruption of megasized proportions that resulted in a destructive column of scalding hot volcanic ash that ultimately reached a stunning height of 80,000 feet. Incredibly, at one point the sound reverberations of blast may have equaled, if not surpassed, the speed of sound. Moreover, it devastated an area 19 miles long by 23 miles wide, and flattened an astonishing 230 square miles of old forest. Sadly, and probably inevitably, those living in the area who chose to stay put didn't stand a chance: Almost 60 deaths, most of them mercifully instantaneous, were recorded. In terms of the local animal populations, around 5,000 deer were killed, as were more than a thousand elk and roughly 12 million salmon. But what of Bigfoot? Did it pay the ultimate price at the hands of nature, too?

BODIES AT THE EPICENTER

Loren Coleman, who is without a doubt the world's leading cryptozoologist, has stated that Mount St. Helens, and nearby Mount Hood and Mount Shasta, act as "lightning rods" for people seeking out Bigfoot, chiefly because the area has a long history of encounters with the famous monster of the woods. Coleman also notes that tales of Bigfoot bodies being found and then covertly removed from the mountain by elements of the U.S. military and forestry personnel surfaced right after the calamitous events of May 1980. Trying to demonstrate that the rumors have any degree of validity is quite another matter, however, as Coleman himself openly admits: "I tried to track them down but hit dead end after dead end." Calling the collective tales "the worst kind of rural folklore," Coleman remains highly skeptical of this cryptozoological equivalent of the alleged recovery of alien bodies by the U.S. government in the desert outside of

Mount St. Helens in Washington State: death and destruction for Bigfoot. © U.S. Geological Survey, 1980. Source: Wikipedia

Roswell, New Mexico, in 1947. But could there be more to the matter than mere myth and legend? Maybe. Within cryptozoological circles plenty of tales abound suggesting that such astonishing discoveries and recoveries really did occur (Bowen, 2010).

Researcher Lon Strickler says that in Cowlitz County, Washington State, at one of researcher Ray Crowe's Western Bigfoot meetings, the matter of the Bigfoot bodies of Mount St. Helens was raised, as was the story of a pair of corpses that the Army Corps of Engineers had allegedly secretly removed from the area around eight weeks after the destruction occurred. A similar tale was recounted in 1985 to investigator Bobbie Short, by a veteran of the Vietnam War. The source was a pilot who knew something of military helicopters scouting the mountain and removing the bodies of bears, deer, elk, and an unknown, hair-covered beast with noticeably charred arms.

And then there are the tales suggesting that a secret dredging operation on the Cowlitz River—whose tributary, the Toutle River, was overwhelmed by volcanic mud at the time of the eruption—uncovered the bodies of two dead Bigfoot that had been found partially buried under piles of mud and sand. They were secretly removed and loaded aboard a double-rotor military helicopter that left almost as quickly as it had arrived. Granted, each one of these tales is brief in the extreme, but when addressed collectively, they do suggest that there may be an actual fire behind all of this smoke.

Earthquakes, Bigfoot, and the U.S. Geological Survey

Perhaps demonstrating evidence that Bigfoot can, like certain other animals, anticipate looming natural disasters, there is a snippet of a tale concerning a National Guard helicopter pilot who maintained that he witnessed a group of seven or more Bigfoots seemingly fleeing the ill-fated mountain in a southwesterly direction only days before the devastating eruption occurred, and while the localized earthquakes were still taking place. Rather intriguingly, the matter of animals clearly reacting (oftentimes in a frenzy) to earthquakes is a phenomenon that certain elements of the U.S. government have taken a deep interest in over the course of many a decade.

For example, documentation prepared by the U.S. Geological Survey—which, notably, was instrumental in warning those living near the site of the eruption to leave the area—states in official documentation:

> *The earliest reference we have to unusual animal behavior prior to a significant earthquake is from Greece in 373*

BC. *Rats, weasels, snakes, and centipedes reportedly left their homes and headed for safety several days before a destructive earthquake. Anecdotal evidence abounds of animals, fish, birds, reptiles, and insects exhibiting strange behavior anywhere from weeks to seconds before an earthquake. However, consistent and reliable behavior prior to seismic events, and a mechanism explaining how it could work, still eludes us* ("Animals & Earthquake Prediction," 2009).

Nevertheless, the USGS has been careful to keep itself informed of any and all advances in this intriguing, albeit poorly understood area of research into some of the decidedly stranger realms of animal behavior. Noting that virtually all creatures possess keen instincts that enable them to flee whenever and wherever predators loom, agency staff have studied the possibility that such "early-warning" behavioral patterns just might allow them to sense the subliminal events or conditions that are associated with impending earthquakes—for example, the slight but significant changes in both the electrical and magnetic fields that we are unable to detect in the slightest.

Even more notably, there is a story that traces a direct connection between the USGS, earthquakes, and Bigfoot. It comes from Dr. Chip Hardesty, who had occasion to meet with a USGS employee who, in 2007, was involved in monitoring seismic activity in the Three Sisters region of Oregon. (The Three Sisters are huge, volcanic peaks in excess of 10,000 feet in the even-more-imposing Cascade Range.) According to Hardesty's source, he encountered a huge, approximately 10-feet-tall Bigfoot—with red hair, no less—crossing a stretch of roads in the area. Though the man had worked in that particular area for around 20 years, he had never previously encountered anything so amazingly weird. Could it be that the beast had sensed the seismic activity that was afoot, which had then caused it to break cover and flee the area, just in case the worst happened and its territory was decimated? That the USGS has exhibited long and undeniable interest in how animals seem to have an innate warning system that alerts them to impending earthquakes and other natural disasters makes that very same agency's link to Bigfoot and its potential response to seismic activity in and around the Three Sisters area even more thought-provoking.

AN UNHOLY ALLIANCE

Bringing matters more up to date, in September 2012, the incredible—and, admittedly, controversial—testimony surfaced of a former National Guardsman who claimed to have been present at Mt. St. Helens when the alleged recovery by the military of a number of Bigfoot bodies took place back in May 1980. Maintaining that he was part of a dedicated cleanup team on the mountain, the unfortunately anonymous source stated that it was not just dead bodies that were found: *Living specimens* were reportedly uncovered, too. The man claimed that after being warned by a member of the military to forget everything that he might see or hear while on duty, he and several colleagues were ordered to wait in a nearby Jeep in an area where they had made camp. After a half an hour or so went by, another Jeep pulled up, and a man in civilian clothes got out and proceeded into a nearby tent. There was nothing strange about that—except when the man exited the tent, lumbering alongside him was what can only be described as a Bigfoot, which apparently displayed significant evidence of major burns to its body. After this astonishing sight, there came an even more amazing development.

Incredibly, the bulky creature clambered into the back of a parked truck, along with the man in the suit, and the astonished National Guardsman and his group were ordered to follow. On five occasions they stopped, always in the vicinity of burned, forested areas dotted with caves, and the same thing happened each time: Both man and beast exited the truck, and the latter issued strange vocalizations in the immediate directions of the caves and woods, almost as if it were calling to its own kind in concerned fashion. This may have been exactly what was going on, because, at two of the five sites, inchoate animalistic replies were heard: one was from an injured creature that was rescued, the other from a creature so severely burned that there was no choice but to put it out of its misery with a swift bullet to the head. Once they returned to camp, the guardsman and his comrades were once again advised that they should keep their mouths firmly shut regarding everything they had just seen and heard. In a field filled with outrageous and unverifiable claims, this one surely has to be near the top of the list. Regardless, it has quickly become a staple part of the legend of the Bigfoot bodies of Mount St. Helens, so I think it deserves to at least be highlighted here and kept on file. That goes for all the other data that appears in this particular story, as well.

Yes, these accounts are fascinating. Yes, they suggest a highly orchestrated project to recover and hide the bodies of at least several dead and injured Bigfoot, and possibly even to assist them, if the 2012 testimony of our mysterious National Guardsman can be trusted. And yes, the U.S.

government seems to have done its utmost to prevent any of this information from getting into the hands of the general public. But here's the problem that faces the cryptozoological research community: Not a single, solitary source that has commented on their alleged direct involvement in, or knowledge of, the matter has gone on the record with his or her full name or background data revealed. That does not mean the entire case lacks merit. It does, however, suggest that when it comes to Bigfoot, we should always note the differences between what we know to be provable fact and that which inhabits a realm filled with rumor, hearsay, and furtive whispers.

CHAPTER 19

THE NESSIE FILES

About 250 million years ago, a huge rift formed across much of Scotland that today goes by the name of the Great Glen. Over the course of the millennia that followed, the gigantic Glen filled with water, the landscape was sculpted anew, and three large lakes were formed: Loch Oich, Loch Lochy, and, the most famous and largest of all, Loch Ness. In excess of 20 miles in length, around a mile wide, and 700 feet deep in places, it is surrounded by dense trees and massive, imposing slopes. It also happens to be the home of one of the world's most famous mystery animals: Nessie, the Loch Ness Monster—or, more correctly, since sightings extend back hundreds of years, Loch Ness *Monsters*. Indeed, for sightings to have continued for so long, the very idea of there being just a single, solitary large creature roaming the dark depths of the loch is absurd in the extreme. If something strange that is made of flesh and blood really does

The British government takes note of the Loch Ness Monster. By Heinrich Harder, 1916.
Source: Wikipedia

lurk deep in the waters of Loch Ness, a herd (school?) of beasts is the only real possibility available to us if we are to explain the ongoing presence and reports.

There's another, seldom-discussed side to the phenomenon of Nessie that is most worthy of our scrutiny: For decades, British government civil servants and military personnel have exhibited far more than passing interest in the monsters of the infamous loch. As for the reasons why, they are just about as strange as they are intriguing. And it all began back in the 1960s with something called the Joint Air Reconnaissance Intelligence Center, or JARIC.

FREAKY FOOTAGE AND THE ROYAL AIR FORCE

Today, JARIC is known as the National Imagery Exploitation Center, which is an integral part of the British Ministry of Defense's Intelligence Collection Group, which operates out of Royal Air Force Brampton, situated in the English county of Cambridgeshire. Although the name of the organization has changed since the 1960s, its role, largely, has not. It has a mandate to analyze photographs and film footage that might have a bearing on the defense of the country, such as the missile bases, military aircraft, and weapons systems of potentially hostile nations. On more than a few occasions in the 1960s, JARIC spent considerable time and effort studying footage that just maybe suggested there really was something large and terrifying swimming in the depths of Loch Ness, and perhaps there still is.

Since the work of JARIC was, for the most part, highly classified in nature, this begs an important question: How was it that JARIC's staff agreed to get involved in the controversy concerning Nessie? Simple: It all came down to an influential person with an equally influential background. David James was a man with a great enthusiasm for the Loch Ness Monster. With one of the founders of the World Wildlife Fund, Sir Peter Scott, he created the Loch Ness Phenomena Investigation Bureau in 1962. But James was much more than just a Nessie enthusiast. During the Second World War he commanded what the British Royal Navy called Motor Gun Boats, and from 1959 to 1964 he served in the British Parliament. Thus, having significant government and military connections, and recognizing that JARIC could assist in the quest for the truth about the Loch Ness Monster, James set the wheels in motion. The rest, as they say, was history: The British military found itself on nothing less than a full-blown monster hunt.

In October of 1962, James traveled to the legendary lake with a number of people from a monster-seeking group called the Loch Ness Investigative Bureau (LNIB). They managed to catch on black-and-white film something that gave every impression of being a large, living animal breaking the surface of the waters. Thanks to James's door-opening abilities, only a few months later JARIC's finest took a careful and close look at the film and stated that it did *not* show a mere wave, as skeptics had loudly and confidently suggested. Rather, the conclusion of the British military's finest photographic analysts was that the LNIB team had captured for posterity a dark, solid object with a surface that glistened. This was, to be sure, a significant development in the Nessie controversy. And that was only the beginning of things.

In August 1965, a woman named Elizabeth Hall filmed nine seconds of something unusual moving in the loch that most assuredly did not appear to be a boat, a seal, or a sturgeon, all three of which have been suggested as potential candidates for images of the Loch Ness Monster. David James again contacted JARIC, and an investigation soon followed. Notably, JARIC's personnel recorded that a careful study of the footage provided by Elizabeth Hall showed clear evidence of *two* wakes, rather than the anticipated one, around 9 feet apart from each other. The mystery of those two wakes and what caused them was never solved. The most amazing development of all, however, came shortly before Christmas 1965, but revolved around something that had occurred half a decade earlier.

On the morning of April 23, 1960, Tim Dinsdale, a well-known seeker of Nessie, filmed something unusual in the waters of the legendary loch. In Dinsdale's very own words: "It lay motionless on the water, a long oval shape, a distinct mahogany color, and on the left flank a huge dark blotch could be seen, like the dapple on a cow." He added, somewhat incongruously, "[f]or some reason it reminded me of the back of an

African buffalo." That Dinsdale had filmed the object for several whole minutes meant that JARIC really had something to get its teeth into. In 1965 it did exactly that, and came up with some remarkable conclusions (Dinsdale, 1989). Stating that whatever it was that Dinsdale caught on film "appears to submerge" at one point, JARIC's staff added: "One can presumably rule out the idea that it is any sort of submarine vessel for various reasons which leaves the conclusion that it is probably an animate object." And, when the statement was made public, and the realization hit home as to who, exactly, had come to such a conclusion (no less than the finest photoanalysts of the British military), many a believer was quickly born and more than a few doubters were converted (Joint Air Reconnaissance Intelligence Center, 1965).

The Prime Minister's monstrous plans

In the late 1970s, documents made available to the public via the Freedom of Information Act (FOIA) reveal that the then–newly elected Conservative government of Prime Minister Margaret Thatcher seriously considered the idea of using dolphins in an extensive search for the legendary beasts of the loch. If the existence of the monsters could be proved, the official world thought, it would have a very positive bearing upon Scotland's tourist industry. No one—believer or skeptic—would doubt that! To keep the media at bay, the government quietly and diplomatically approached the Scottish Society for the Prevention of Cruelty to Animals in order to get their views on the matter, but complaints from the Society put the brakes on the ambitious plan, so it was never put into action. Still, the Nessie File remained open.

In 1985, clearly exhibiting an ongoing fascination with the monsters of Loch Ness, the Iron Lady's government secretly tried to determine if the animals might be at risk from hunters and poachers, either then or at some point in the future. At one point, government officials actually mused upon the idea of drafting new legislation to protect the Nessie or Nessies, creatures no one could be sure even existed in the first place. Eventually, as FOIA-declassified documents show, the government concluded that "[t]he legislative framework to protect the monster is available; provided she (or he) is identified by scientists whose reputation will carry weight with the British Museum" (Horne, 2006).

So far, no such identification of what swims in the waters of Loch Ness has ever been formally made. Unless, that is, someone, somewhere deep in the heart of the British government knows something that the rest of us don't know—which, given what we have seen thus far on the matter of monsters and official secrecy, would not exactly be surprising news if it ever became public knowledge. It's not just the British government that has taken a keen interest in Nessie, however; the U.S. government's Department of the Interior has had its eyes and ears focused on the mysteries of Loch Ness, too.

INTEREST IN NESSIE ACROSS THE POND

A 1977 report demonstrates that the DoI knew a great deal about the history of, and theories concerning, the beast of the loch:

> *"Nessie," as the creature is affectionately known by believers in its existence, has been periodically sighted in Loch Ness, Scotland, over the last 14 centuries. But the most*

　　　MONSTER FILES

recent reports, based on sophisticated underwater cam-
eras and electronic gear, identify a 30-foot-long creature
with a massive, humped body bearing a small head and
long slender neck with an immense set of flippers ("Are We
Ready for 'Bigfoot' or the Loch Ness Monster?" 1977).

The DoI added that, although in 1977 there were no creatures in Loch Ness—or indeed anywhere on the planet—that
looked like this, the general description attributed to Nessie
"would fit any of various species of prehistoric, carnivorous
reptiles called plesiosaurs which lived 100 million years ago"
(Ibid.). Regarding the matter of officialdom and the monster, the
DoI noted that "[i]n recent discussion in the British House of
Commons, members of Parliament were assured that if 'Nessie'
were found it could theoretically receive immediate protection
since it had already been described and named" (Ibid.) Having
clearly spent much time pondering the creature and its nature
and possible classification, the DoI added that in the event a
specimen of the monster was secretly captured and smuggled
out of the loch and brought to the United States, it would be a
serious and direct violation of the U.S. Lacey Act, which was
created in 1900 to prevent the illegal transport of animals and
plants into the mainland United States (Ibid.).

From the elite of the Royal Air Force to Prime Minister
Margaret Thatcher, and from the British House of Commons
to the heart of the U.S. government, the Loch Ness Monster
has attracted far more than its fair share of official interest
and intrigue. A bureaucratic beast, to be sure!

CHAPTER 20

A NIGHTMARE FROM THE SKIES

We have already seen how, in the early 1960s, staff at NASA's John H. Glenn Research Center at Lewis Field, Ohio, were involved in a deeply weird saga that reportedly began with the sighting of anomalous aerial phenomena in the immediate vicinity of the installation, and ended in the shooting, slaying, and autopsying of nothing less than a Bigfoot—all of which suggests the beast was far stranger than just a giant ape of the unclassified kind. This is not the only time the U.S. government's space agency has crossed paths with uncanny, nightmarish beasts. For what might be a perfect example of this, we need to go back to the 1980s and the heart of NASA's Johnson Space Center in Houston, Texas, where something infernal was trolling the night skies right over the facility.

The Mothman takes a vacation

On 11 known occasions, during the darkening months of the late autumn and early winter of 1986, staff at the center reported something disturbing and sensational: sightings of what bore an uncanny resemblance to the winged terror in the *Jeepers Creepers* movies, or perhaps the legendary Mothman of Point Pleasant, West Virginia, which became the subject of John's Keel's much-praised book, *The Mothman Prophecies*, as

A winged beast and secret files.
By Edward Newman, 1843. Source: Wikipedia

well as the 2002 movie of the same name. The Mothman was a winged, shining-eyed entity that allegedly haunted Point Pleasant in the 1960s and sparked a panic in the people of the town. And its cousin in the Lone Star State did exactly that at the Johnson Space Center years later—hardly surprising, given that the monster was described as having shiny, oily-looking black skin, a pair of huge, batlike, membranous wings, and, perhaps most memorable and unsettling of all, a long, flowing black cape of the type that would have made the world's most legendary vampire, Count Dracula himself, envious to the extreme.

Intriguingly, every one of these encounters took place late at night, and involved staff working late shifts who had the opportunity to see the creature as they were arriving, leaving, or, in the case of security personnel, patrolling the facility. In addition, the weather was always the same: chilly temperature, clear skies empty of clouds, and a wild, howling wind. Really, all that was missing was a pack of supernatural hounds, a witch on a broomstick, and a full moon!

One night in November 1986, in what was arguably the most terrifying encounter, several of the witnesses (including two guards on patrol) spotted the winged fiend squatting on its haunches on the roof of a small storage building before soaring upward into the starry night with astonishing speed. The witnesses also described an uncanny sensation or energy of profound malevolence fairly oozing from the creature; it seemed to enjoy and actually bask sadistically in the knowledge that it had been seen and had provoked so much fear and dread in the witnesses. Afterward, such was the level of wild anxiety and rampant rumor that spread around certain parts of the facility that an official, albeit low-key investigation was launched, in which security personnel took statements from the witnesses. What else could they have done, particularly given the fact that most of the accounts didn't surface for days, or even weeks after they occurred? Not much—until the next dramatic and, this time, deadly development in the story occurred.

Shortly before Christmas 1986, the torn-apart and—as subsequent autopsies demonstrated—nearly bloodless corpses of two German Shepherds were found onsite, at the edge of a staff parking area, right around where the flying menace had been seen only four nights previously. In this case, the investigation was taken to a whole new level. The reason was obvious: If dogs were being slaughtered by the creature, then might the staff itself be next on the lethal list? It was a sobering thought that led police and, briefly, even the local FBI office to become involved in the investigation. The probe ultimately led only to a dead end, largely as a result of the fact that by early January 1987, the sightings had ceased. Moreover, despite discreet inquiries with local veterinarians, the owners of the two unfortunate dogs were never located. The flying fiend had seemingly moved on to pastures new, and the staff of the Johnson Space Center that was in on the story could finally breathe a big, collective sigh of relief.

Certainly, this is a decidedly strange and sinister story that relies solely on the testimony of two former employees at the center who, approximately a quarter of a century after the events occurred, have been willing to share at least the basics of what took place. But what about the beast? Do we have any way of truly knowing what it was, and why its target of interest was NASA? Well, we may not be able to identify what the winged *thing* was, but it can be said with certainty that this was not the only occasion when Houston was plagued by such a terrible flying entity of the night. Nor was it the only time that a facility intimately linked to space exploration had a cloaked monster in its midst that had an evil and savage predilection for mutilating animals in such a horrific fashion. To demonstrate this, we have to go further into Houston's history—back to the summer of 1953, to be precise.

Houston's beastly batman

Less than a year after the 12-foot-tall, flying (or floating) monster of Flatwoods, West Virginia, put in its legendary appearance for a handful of folk in the town, something very similar occurred in the heart of the Texan city of Houston. Whether or not we can lay this later, and particularly beastly, affair squarely on the shoulders of the U.S. Air Force's psychological warfare planners and the strange Second World War–era mind games of Jasper Maskelyne, is debatable. But as we'll see, there are undeniable similarities that must give us at least some food for thought. Or, if it *wasn't* a weird tool of government, but something truly unknown, perhaps the 1950s fiend of Texas was the very same one that popped up three decades later at the nearby Houston Space Center.

It all began shortly after midnight on June 18, 1953, on what was a torturously hot and steamy night in the city. It was one of those nights that makes sleep practically impossible without good air-conditioning, which is why 23-year-old Hilda Walker and a couple of her neighbors, Howard Phillips and Judy Meyer, were sitting on her East Third Street porch, sweaty, restless, and miserable. They were looking for some relief from the heat, but, as matters transpired, that was to be the absolute least of their worries. Walker spelled out how the calamitous events began. As the trio sat and chatted, "25 feet away I saw a huge shadow across the lawn. I thought at first it was the magnified reflection of a big moth caught in the nearby street light. Then the shadow seemed to bounce upward into a pecan tree. We all looked up. That's when we saw it" ("Unearthly Batman Terrifies Watchers," 1953). "It" was a very simple yet apt term to use. Walker described an encounter with something that appeared to be an unholy combination of the Mothman and the horror of the Houston Space Center. (N.b. This was long before either was on anyone's radar.) The creature may have been humanoid in shape, but it was clearly far from human. Utterly black, and with the ubiquitous batlike wings, it was an estimated 7 feet tall and was bathed in an eerie, yellowish glow. As soon as she saw it, Meyer screamed in terror at the top of her lungs. Who can blame her for that?

Walker, clearly the most forthcoming of the three, described what happened next to the local press (who were of course overjoyed by the sensational story):

> *Immediately afterwards, we heard a loud swoosh over the house tops across the street. It was like the white flash of a torpedo-shaped object.... I've heard so much about flying saucer stories and I thought all those people telling the stories were crazy, but now I don't know what to believe. I may be nuts, but I saw it, whatever it was.... I sat there stupefied. I was amazed* (Gerhard, 2010).

Cryptozoologist Ken Gerhard, who spent a number of years living in Houston, has documented several cases very similar to that of Walker, Meyer, and Phillips, including one that occurred as recently as the 1990s. The time was, yet again, the dead of night, and the location was the rooftop of Houston's Bellaire Theater, where a "gigantic, helmeted man" with wings was seen by petrified staff. Perhaps, speculates Gerhard, the flying monster has never really left, and still dwells in the darker, shadowy parts of the old city (Ibid.).

Terror at the telescope

In the late 1950s an historic document, bearing the title *Searching for Interstellar Communications*, was prepared by Phillip Morrison and Giuseppe Conconi, a pair of physicists at Cornell University, and was published within the prestigious pages of *Nature*. Its focus: the potential feasibility of seeking out alien life via high-powered microwaves. The paper received a great deal of interest, particularly from a man named Frank Drake, who chose to turn the theories of Morrison and Conconi into reality at the Green Bank National Radio Astronomy Observatory in West Virginia, home to two of the world's most infamous flying creatures: Mothman and the Flatwoods Monster. Despite a lack of success, Drake pressed on. In October 1961, a conference (what became known as the Search for Extraterrestrial Intelligence, or SETI) was held at Green Bank. Drake proved to be the standout character, when he revealed to the audience what has famously become known as the Drake Equation—a theoretical means of determining the number of intelligent alien cultures that might exist in the known universe.

At this point, it's worth noting that NASA and SETI, although separate entities, are hardly strangers. In 1971, for example, Project Cyclops, a NASA think tank that was created to address the matter of how a gigantic array of radio telescopes might be used to locate extraterrestrial life, had significant input from SETI. Similarly, there is also a link between dark-cloaked, vampiric entities and shocking cases of animal mutilation. When Frank Drake chose to focus his work on a quest for extraterrestrial life, it was a decision that ultimately took him to Puerto Rico and its now-famous Arecibo Radio Telescope, of which Drake ultimately rose to the rank of director. Notably, sometime during the 1960s, a security guard at Arecibo reported seeing a black-cloaked figure walking along a narrow trail on the perimeter of the huge telescope. For the guard, this was no local or trespasser; it was a feaster of blood: a fully fledged vampire. Drake, although skeptical, was not about to deny that at least *something* had prompted the guard to report his experience, and so he requested that a written account be provided to him, which it duly was. Two days later, Drake said, "I really was forced to look into it...because a cow was found dead on a nearby farm, with all the blood drained from its body. The vampire rumor had already spread through the observatory staff, and now the cow incident whipped the fears of many people into a frenzy" (Drake, 1994).

Was it simply chance or random coincidence that cloaked monsters were seen at both the Arecibo Observatory on the island of Puerto Rico in the mid-1960s, and at NASA's Johnson Space Center at Houston, Texas, in 1986—monsters that went on to become forever linked to the violent slaughter of animals whose blood appeared to have been completely drained from their bodies? Should the files on those gruesome cases ever be released into the public domain, maybe one day we will finally have an answer to that puzzling and unsettling question.

CHAPTER 21

SPECTERS AND PHANTIMALS

Despite the fact that there have been literally thousands of sightings of Bigfoot within the forests of North America, spanning a period of at least several centuries, each and every attempt to identify, trap, or kill even one such animal has ended in complete and utter failure. Unlike just about every other animal in the United States, no Bigfoot has ever had the misfortune of being hit by a car or truck and killed, nor has anyone ever stumbled across the corpse of one of these elusive animals. Though there are countless cases on record in which people have attempted to shoot a Bigfoot, the bullets seem to have no effect whatsoever on the animals. It's much the same with the monster (or monsters) of Loch Ness. Although the loch is sizeable, it is hardly remote or inaccessible. Tens of thousands of people flock to Scotland every year in hopes of spotting one of the elusive, long-necked creatures of those dark waters. Practically all of them go home disappointed. Ambitious projects designed to locate the creatures with sonar and submarines have proven inconclusive. Attempts to photograph the animals on the rare occasions they have surfaced from the murky depths have often proved to be curiously problematic: Eyewitnesses report cameras that jam at crucial moments, and photographs that are inexplicably blurred or fogged when developed.

And then there's the matter of the eating habits of these mysterious beasts—or, more correctly, their overwhelming *lack* of eating habits. Given its immense size and build, Bigfoot, for example, would likely require a massive intake of food on a daily basis. After all, a fully grown silverback gorilla requires an average of 45 pounds of food *per day*—and that's just for one animal! Imagine the amount of nourishment required by a whole colony of silverbacks. Indeed, one of the reasons why it is so easy to track the movements and activities of gorillas is the clear and undeniable evidence of their constant, massive foraging for food. Bigfoot rarely, if ever, demonstrates such evidence of its culinary delights. Yes, there are rare reports of Bigfoot killing a pig here or a deer there, but for the most part the hard evidence of its eating habits—which would have to be absolutely tremendous, considering the eyewitness reports describing creatures reaching heights of 8 feet and weights of an estimated 300 to 600 pounds—is inexplicably lacking. That Bigfoot is seen in locales hardly noted for their rich and abundant food supplies, such as the arid wilds of the Nevada desert and West Texas, only adds to the ever-present high strangeness.

A similar situation exists at Loch Ness. If a large colony of plesiosaurs has managed to survive extinction and now calls the loch its home, how, exactly, are the animals sustaining their massive bulks? Yes, the loch is populated by a number of fish, such as salmon, eel, pike and trout, but the populations of these fish are most assuredly not in the numbers that would allow a school or herd of, say, 20 beasts, each 15 to 20 feet in length, to secure sufficient daily nourishment to ensure their survival, health, and reproduction over the centuries or even eons. So, while most (if not all) cryptozoological beasts initially appear to be real, flesh-and-blood animals—albeit ones that are yet to be classified by science—upon careful study, their curious eating habits and activities suggest they are actually nothing of the sort. Indeed, they seem rather more spectral, ethereal, and phantomlike. Could it be that some of the strange and fantastic monsters that plague and perplex people all across the world on dark, windswept nights, within thick woods, and amid the cold waters of ancient lochs and lakes are far less or, paradoxically, far more than they appear to be?

THE "PHANTIMAL" PHENOMENON

When we chatted in 2010 about such matters, paranormal expert Joshua P. Warren, the author of *Pet Ghosts*, told me that he had extensively investigated a series of bizarre encounters with apparitional ancient animals on farmland in Lancaster, South Carolina, one of which seemed to resemble a ghostly pterodactyl. Josh told me that he had entertained the possibility that the ghostly presence of certain extinct animals may very well help explain at least *some* sightings of monstrous beasts, particularly those that seemingly appear and vanish in the blink of an eye. Joshua calls such beasts *phantimals*.

"Maybe Bigfoot is a phantimal," said Josh, "perhaps even the ghost of a prehistoric creature, similar to the enormous extinct possible ape, *Gigantopithecus*, or maybe even the spirits

Paranormal sleuth Joshua P. Warren believes some monsters may be ghosts.
© Nick Redfern, 2007.

of primitive humans." He went on to explain that he was not adverse to the idea that the world's most famous lake-monster, our old friend Nessie (an obsession of the government of British Prime Minister Margaret Thatcher) might actually represent some form of "ghostly plesiosaur," rather than an actual living animal or even a colony of animals. Amazingly, the U.S. government just might be in agreement with Warren (Redfern, 2010).

Spies and specters

While digging deep into the subject of officialdom's secret research into the realms of so-called remote viewing and psychic spying, Jim Marrs, one of the world's leading experts on conspiracy theories, learned that elements of the officialdom had attempted to solve the riddle of what lurks under the surface of Loch Ness. According to Marrs, several remote-viewing sessions that targeted the Loch Ness Monster actually revealed physical traces of the beast—such as a wake in the water or the distinct movement of a large body beneath the surface of the loch. Significantly, those involved in the remote viewing of Loch Ness even made drawings of long-necked, humpbacked animals that eerily resembled the presumed extinct plesiosaurs of previous eras. However, as Marrs noted, when the government's remote viewers attempted to dig deeper into the puzzle, they hit upon a startling discovery: The creatures—if that is what they really were—seemed to have the strange ability to appear and then vanish, like ghosts, into thin air. Marrs had this to say on the curious development in the affair of Nessie: "Considering that reports of human ghosts date back throughout man's history, the Psi Spies seriously considered the possibility that the Loch Ness Monster is nothing less than a dinosaur's ghost" (Marrs, 2000).

Bunny RIP

A U.S. Defense Intelligence Agency document dating from September 1975 titled *Soviet and Czechoslovakian Parapsychological Research*, which has been declassified under the terms of the United States' Freedom of Information Act, reveals a wealth of interest on the part of the American military in the research of a Soviet doctor named Pavel Naumov, as it related to life after death in the animal kingdom. Somewhat disturbingly, the document states:

Dr. Naumov conducted studies between a submerged Soviet Navy submarine and a shore research station:

these tests involved a mother rabbit and her newborn litter and occurred around 1956. According to Naumov, Soviet scientists placed the baby rabbits aboard the submarine. They kept the mother rabbit in a laboratory on shore where they implanted electrodes in her brain. When the submarine was submerged, assistants killed the rabbits one by one. At each precise moment of death, the mother rabbit's brain produced detectable and recordable reactions (Maire III, 1975).

Far more significantly, American military spies, writing in 1975 noted that "[a]s late as 1970 the precise protocol and results of this test described by Naumov were believed to be classified." Clearly, this official document—classified Top Secret and circulated amongst the highest echelons of the United States' defense and intelligence communities— demonstrates undeniable military interest in the nature of the afterlife within the animal kingdom (Ibid.).

A second copy of this document, declassified in 2007 by the National Security Agency (NSA), includes a very intriguing, albeit brief, handwritten notation on the document, which states in part: "A better understanding of Naumov's work might make our 'Bigfoot' archives clearer. Can Wenner look into this further?" (Ibid.) Despite persistent digging, precisely what the NSA's "Bigfoot archives" may represent, and who Wenner was or still is, remain a mystery. However, that someone within the NSA had made a connection between Naumov's work on animal souls, spirits, and the Bigfoot conundrum is intriguing to say the very least.

Perhaps elements of the U.S. government know something we don't about animals—of both the known and unknown variety—cryptozoology, and the afterlife. Maybe they are fully aware that lake monsters and Bigfoot are not the flesh-and-blood creatures they appear to be, but the beastly dead returned to life.

CHAPTER 22

THE ABCS OF A ROYAL CONSPIRACY

In the late 1980s, English monster-hunter Jonathan Downes became personally embroiled in a controversy that began with the investigation of a mysterious large cat or cats on the loose in Britain, and which ultimately extended into the heart of the British monarchy, military, and government, and the domain of deep and dark official secrecy. Unbelievably, the most significant part of the story had to do with the secret love life of the late Diana, Princess of Wales. For decades—possibly for centuries—the British Isles have played host to a peculiar breed of mystery animal. They are the so-called Alien Big Cats—ABCs, as they have become infamously known. It scarcely needs mentioning that Britain is not currently home to an indigenous species of large cat, black or tan in color, and the size of a fully grown mountain lion or larger, as hundreds of witnesses steadfastly assert they have seen. Nevertheless, amazing stories have circulated from all across the nation concerning sightings of large, predatory cats that savagely feed on both livestock and wild animals, and that amaze, intrigue, and terrify the populace in the process.

Their memorable monikers include the Beast of Dartmoor, the Essex Lion, the Surrey Puma, and the Beast of Bodmin. What they really are, however, is quite another issue entirely. Some people believe that they are escapees from circuses and zoos; others suggest they are exotic pets that have broken out of private enclosures; and yet others take the incredible and highly controversial stance that—against all the odds and accepted wisdom—Britain really is home to an indigenous large cat that has successfully avoided capture and classification for as long as people have inhabited those ancient isles. While the theories concerning the existence of these cats are many, persuasive eyewitness testimony offers us some significant answers that point in only one particular direction.

Confessions of the Lion Man

If someone had said to me that before I embarked upon my quest for the truth about the big cats of Britain back in the 1990s, I would find myself digging into the accounts of a man known as the Lion Man and his pal, One-Eyed Nick Maiden— whose moniker made him sound like something straight out of the pages of Treasure Island or the latest installment of the *Pirates of the Caribbean* franchise—I would probably have merely smiled and forgotten all about it. But sometimes truth really is stranger than fiction. England's Lion Man, Louis Foley, claimed to have been personally acquainted with a number of people who had stealthily released big cats into the heart of England's expansive Cannock Chase woods in the 1970s, largely as a result of the significant changes that were made around that time to the Dangerous Wild Animals Act, which regulates the keeping of exotic animals in the United Kingdom. I met Foley midway through 2000, when I was coauthoring a column on strange mysteries for a now defunct English newspaper called the *Chase Post*. His fascination with big cats began back in the 1970s, when he purchased his first lion, ostensibly to function as a guard dog.

Astonishingly, Foley's burgeoning interest eventually resulted in his possessing a veritable zoo of exotic big cats, including seven lions, tigers, pumas, panthers, and even a crocodile. According to Foley's personal recollections of that long-gone era,

> *[h]eartless cowards who bought panthers and other big cats as fashion accessories soon realized what a handful they could be. They were left to die in areas like the Chase and many of them would have perished because they were tame. But I have seen tracks and evidence of kills that proves there are many that survived* ("More than 100 pumas and leopards may be at large in Britain," 2000).

A SECRET CALL FROM A SOLDIER

Jonathan Downes has investigated many reports of what may very well be examples of big cats released into the wild, reports that seem to support what was revealed by Louis Foley. Downes's home county of Devonshire is dominated by wild and windswept foggy moors, rolling hills, and dense woods—the ideal

Monster-hunter Jonathan Downes: an investigator of big cat conspiracies. © Nick Redfern, 2010.

territory in which big cats could easily dwell and hunt in safety and stealth. Downes himself is convinced that the marauding beasts really are, in the words of *The X-Files*, out there. With that in mind, let us now delve deeply into the heart of a very strange conspiracy of the curious, cat kind that crossed Downes's path and that plunged him into a world of uncertainty, government secrets, and profound paranoia.

Late one night in the late 1980s, Jonathan Downes received a mysterious, conspiratorial telephone call from a man who wished to discuss with the famous monster hunter his personal knowledge of big cat activity in the southwest of England, the area in which Downes has resided since childhood. This caller was quite unlike any other. Back in 1983, the voice at the other end of the phone had been attached to someone in the British military—the Royal Marines, to be specific—which at that time was engaged in a widely publicized search for the legendary, elusive animals. At the time the operation provoked massive media coverage, both locally and nationally. After all, it wasn't every day that the British public saw fully armed troops roaming the land by day and night in search of fantastic beasts. The official story is that the cats, if they really were out there, skillfully avoided detection, capture, or killing on each and every occasion. Downes's new mystery source suggested something quite different, however.

As Downes listened carefully, an astonishing tale unfolded. The Royal Marines actually did find evidence of big cats roaming the wild landscape. Not on public land, but on the fringes of the private estate of a rich and powerful landowner late one dark, shadowy night. Supposedly, one junior member of the military contingent panicked at the sight of a trio of large, black cats of unknown type and origin roaming around, at which point he unleashed a salvo of bullets that brought their lives to a sudden, violent, and bloody end. Since the troops had inadvertently trespassed onto private property and a weapon had been fired, a hasty cover-up was put into place: The bodies of the huge cats were immediately and quietly scooped up by the marines and quickly disposed of. The troops then stealthily left the area, careful to avoid leaving any evidence of their presence, never mind that of the cats. This was far from the end of the story, however.

THE PRINCESS AND THE PANTHER

Downes's Deep Throat source told him that, a few years after the fact, he had been part of a surveillance team that was keeping a close watch on the movements and activities of the late Diana, Princess of Wales, specifically at the time of her affair with Major James Hewitt of the British Army, which is acknowledged as having begun at some point in the summer of 1986. Curiously and coincidentally, Downes actually went to school with Hewitt, which made what the soldier had to say all the more intriguing. It should be stressed that Downes's informant related his story years before the truth of the Diana-Hewitt relationship sensationally surfaced on British television in 1995, when Diana herself finally confirmed the rumors that were circulating. Of course, this adds even more credibility to Downes's source.

According to what Downes was told, on one occasion, when the unit was keeping watch on Diana as she spent a secret night at Hewitt's home in the Devonshire village of Bratton Clovelly—a place Downes knew, and still knows, very well—the soldiers, whose job it was to ensure that the princess did not become a victim of terrorist groups such as the Irish Republican Army (IRA), encountered a huge black cat prowling around the area at the very same time they had their night-vision equipment focused on Diana and Hewitt. The soldiers were suddenly plunged into a deep quandary: If they killed the huge beast, all hell would break loose, Hewitt and Diana would be alerted to the fact that they were being covertly watched by the elite of the British military—almost certainly on the secret orders of certain powerful figures at Buckingham Palace, the intelligence community, or both—and the press would soon be hot on the trail of a royal scandal of massive proportions.

So the soldiers took the only reasonable option they felt was open to them: They did nothing at all, aside from silently and anxiously watching as the creature wandered around for a while, eventually moving on from the grounds of Hewitt's property for pastures new and unknown. But, said Downes's informant, he felt it was finally time for the truth to come out about Britain's big cats and what the military secretly knew about the matter. And although those skeptical of such a sensational story might suggest that the alleged whistleblower was just some deranged fantasist, it's worth noting the following words of Downes himself on this matter, which back up one of the most important aspects of this story: "It must be said in his defense that he told me this long before the liaison [between Hewitt and Diana] became public knowledge. It was certainly the first time I had heard of the scandal that was, years later, to rock both the nation and the monarchy" (Redfern, 2006).

A SPECIAL INVESTIGATION

In early 2006, it was revealed that shortly after Jonathan Downes received his mysterious, late-night call, an elite arm of the British Police Force took a deep interest in the famous creature-seeking author and his big-cat pursuits. The name of this elite unit is Special Branch, and its work typically concerns counter-terrorism. It so transpires that Special Branch had come to a very odd and wholly erroneous conclusion regarding Downes and the story told to him by his clandestine informant, which Downes quickly pursued with understandable enthusiasm and vigor. For a while, Special Branch was concerned that Downes was using the big cat investigation as an ingenious form of camouflage to try and uncover further, damaging information about the royal family, Princess Diana, and James Hewitt, and that he was going to share it all with none other than the highest echelons of the Irish Republican Army (IRA), which of course would lead to a scandal of massive proportions for the British establishment. Was a hunter of monsters on the brink of potentially collapsing the entire British establishment, deliberately or inadvertently? The theory, bizarre but undeniably intriguing, was dropped by Special Branch when intensive digging on the part of its staff revealed that Downes was, and still is, an ardent royalist; that he most assuredly was not a supporter of the IRA; and that he has a brother in the British Army who is a priest and who had been decorated by Queen Elizabeth II, and a father who, while living in Hong Kong in the 1960s, held a position of prominence with the government's Colonial Service. Regardless, Special Branch surveillance of Downes continued.

OWLMAN ATTRACTS THE MEN IN BLACK

The next leg of this strange journey began on a seemingly innocuous early afternoon in May 1996, when Downes was sitting in the departure lounge of England's Plymouth Airport. He was there to say his farewells to a close and dear friend who had been visiting for several days. The friend's name was Tony "Doc" Shiels, a controversial character in cryptozoological circles who also happened to be Irish. Back in the summer of 1976, Shiels gained widespread notoriety when he publicized the bizarre encounters of a number of young girls who claimed to have seen a glowing-eyed, winged beast—described as looking part human and part giant owl—in the woods of Mawnan village, Cornwall, England. Arguably the closest thing that the United Kingdom has to the legendary Mothman of Point Pleasant, it became known as the Owlman.

While Downes and Shiels hung out awaiting the boarding process that would begin Shiels's journey on his way back to his home in Ireland, a classic, grim-faced "Man in Black" character approached Shiels, flashed a police ID card, and demanded to see his boarding pass. All was fortunately in order and the MIB merely scowled ominously and walked away. Downes, wondering what on earth that was all about, made his way to the bathroom and, while in one of the stalls, overheard a conversation between two men that—to Downes's complete and utter consternation and concern—actually revolved around him and Special Branch. Downes only caught brief snippets of what was said, but it was clear that he was still being watched closely by officialdom. Downes's opinion and recollections of the day in question are valuable:

> *I still don't know to this day what it was all about. The harassment, such as it was, continued all afternoon, but we were, by this time at least, in such a state of advanced paranoia that even innocent occurrences were open to vicious misinterpretation. Was the target of this activity me or Tony? Was Tony guilty of being Irish in the wrong place at the wrong time? It was a week when security at all airports and military bases had been stepped up because of a rumored IRA blitz to coincide with the 80th anniversary of the Easter uprising* (Redfern, 2006).

SECRET FILES AND DEATHS AT A ZOO

The strange affair of the man forever linked with the Owlman was over, but the secret and careful scrutiny of Downes's activities in the field of cryptozoology was not. It was also during the 1990s that Downes acquired a collection of photocopies of British Police Force files on the vicious mutilation and killing of animals—including geese and wallabies—at England's Newquay Zoo in 1978. The then-still-classified papers had been secretly given to Downes by a researcher, Joan Amos, who took with her to the grave the secret of exactly how she obtained the stash of *X-Files*–type police reports, which postulated the killings might have been the work of a large, predatory cat of unknown origin and type that, incredibly, had actually forced its way into the zoo! Thus, that Downes had in his possession official, secret documentation on potential big cat attacks in the U.K.—documentation that, at the time, should have been steadfastly held behind the closed doors of Britain's police, and with no public access whatsoever—was yet another reason why the famous monster hunter became such a headache for the agents of Special Branch, the British Army, and, quite possibly, even the elite of the Royal Family itself.

By the time the 20th century came to a close, it seemed that the secret surveillance of Jonathan Downes was finally at an end, as well—much to his eternal relief. However, this was far from being the end of official government interest in Britain's big cats, as will become acutely apparent in later chapters.

CHAPTER 23

THE BIGGEST BLOOPER OF THEM ALL

During the 1960s, the U.S. Navy created and put into place a vast array of underwater microphones, or hydrophones, around virtually the entire the planet. The reason was as simple as it was secret: to keep careful track of the movements of the Soviet Union's fleet of submarines, many of which were armed with sizable numbers of nuclear warheads. The project became known as SOSUS, or Sound Surveillance System. Even though the Cold War is now long over and done with, the listening stations are still in place to this day, hundreds of meters below the surface of the world's oceans, where sound waves become trapped in a layer of water known as the Deep Sound Channel. It's here that temperature and pressure cause sound waves to keep moving without being wildly scattered by the ocean surface or floor. As for those sounds detected by SOSUS, most can be traced back to everyday causes such as whales, ships, and even earthquakes.

The National Oceanic and Atmospheric Administration (NOAA), an agency within the U.S. government's Department of Commerce, undertakes similar work on a routine basis. Back in the summer of 1997, however, things were far from routine. NOAA's Equatorial Pacific Ocean autonomous hydrophone—which was created to augment the Navy's SOSUS program and plays a key role in monitoring populations and migrations of deep-sea animals—detected a strange anomaly at a remote point in the South Pacific Ocean, just west of the southern tip of South America. Depending on whose version of events you accept, the nature of the anomaly suggests that huge, terrifying monsters may be lurking deep in the ocean and that the U.S. government knows a great deal about it.

What the Bloop is it?

Within official circles, the anomaly became infamously known as "Bloop." According to NOAA's records, it lasted around 60 seconds and was of sufficient amplitude to be detected on sensors ranging more than 5,000 kilometers from the site. Not only that, the sonic frequencies that were monitored convinced some within officialdom that if a living, breathing thing really was roaming the waters off South America, as the recordings suggested, then it was clearly bigger than any recognized or categorized creature of the sea. Was a marauding monster of massive proportions on the loose? Had H.P. Lovecraft's terrifying Cthulhu coiled its way out of the realm of horror fiction and into the world of reality?

Those who thought this might be the case felt that the Bloop recording just might be evidence of a giant squid. And we're talking here about the giant of all giants. Certainly, squid can grow to impressive sizes: Current estimates are between 33 and 46 feet, although unverified reports of 60-foot-long monsters do exist. Might Bloop have been an even bigger beast, the definitive granddaddy of the squid world? In the domain of adventurous fiction and science fiction, giant squids reach even more massive sizes—for example, those that took on Captain Nemo and his crew in Jules Verne's classic novel

Beware the deadly, giant squid. By Harper Lee, 1884. Source: Wikipedia

Twenty Thousand Leagues under the Sea; the one that caused death and mayhem in Peter Benchley's *Beast*; and that which provoked terror for the whale-obsessed Captain Ahab in the pages of Herman Melville's acclaimed *Moby-Dick*. Fiction is one thing, but what about fact?

Phil Lobel, a marine biologist at Boston University, was skeptical of the giant squid theory. He noted that cephalopods lack the gas-filled sacs that would enable them to make noise. But Lobel couldn't dismiss his feeling that Bloop, whatever it was, was probably caused by something that was biological in origin. Indeed, Christopher Fox of NOAA's Portland, Oregon facility confirmed that other such anomalies had been recorded over the years all around the planet, and had been given a variety of names, such as Gregorian Chant, Upsweep, Slowdown, Whistle, and Train. Interestingly, Fox did not discount the possibility that the Bloop signal came from a living creature, as its signature was, he explained, somewhat akin to a sped-up variation of sounds made by known and identified animals of the oceans.

Nevertheless, the matter was finally laid to rest—from the perspective of NOAA, at least. The official stance today is that the mysterious sounds recorded in 1997 are not unlike what one would expect to encounter during the fracturing and cracking of large icebergs. NOAA adds that the iceberg they believe caused all the fuss back then was most likely situated somewhere between Brasnfield Straits and the Ross Sea, or possibly at Cape Adare, a well-known source of what are termed *cryogenic signals*. And that's where matters still stand today—unless, of course, you subscribe to the theory that H.P. Lovecraft's fictional Cthulhu is not quite so fictional, after all. Or the theory that the U.S. government is still hiding the truth about terrible, marauding beasts that lurk in the deep, ancient waters of our planet. And speaking of things that lurk in the oceans...

CHAPTER 24

IN SEARCH OF THE GOVERNMENT'S MERMAIDS

In May 2012, the Animal Planet channel broadcast a two-hour-long, prime time show titled *Mermaids: The Body Found*, which also aired one month later on the Discovery Channel. It was an undeniably thrilling and captivating production, presented in documentary format, that suggested the National Oceanic and Atmospheric Administration was up to its neck in a controversy of massive proportions. There was nothing less than a gigantic cover-up in progress, meant to hide the existence of mermaids. Yes, mermaids. But, these were not the sort of creatures that most of us think of when addressing such matters. Rather than being flowing-haired, buxom, exotic women with the lower bodies of fish, they were a savage and violent offshoot of the human race that had turned its back on the land millennia ago and evolved in the oceans. Over hundreds of thousands of years, lungs became gills, feet became webbed, and their overall

Do "mermaids" resembling the Creature from the Black Lagoon lurk in our oceans?
© Nick Refern, 2009.

appearance became that of fearsome things far closer to *The Creature from the Black Lagoon* than curvy Daryl Hannah in *Splash*. Such an improbable theory is far from being a new one, however. It's known as the Aquatic Ape Theory.

MERMAIDS: MYTH OR HOAX?

In the early 1940s, Max Westenhöfer, a pathologist from Germany, famously, and rather controversially said: "The postulation of an aquatic mode of life during an early stage of human evolution is a tenable hypothesis, for which further inquiry may produce additional supporting evidence" (Westenhöfer, 1942). This was echoed nearly 20 years later by one Alister Hardy, a marine biologist who stated his beliefs and conclusions in a forthright manner. His particular theory was one suggesting that a branch of "this primitive ape-stock" had been "forced by competition from life in the trees to feed on the sea-shores and to hunt for food, shell fish, sea-urchins etc., in the shallow waters off the coast. I suppose that they were forced into the water just as we have seen happen in so many other groups of terrestrial animals" (Hardy, 1960). Had the Animal Planet's show vindicated the work of Westenhöfer and Hardy? According to the production, it had. The NOAA had got its hands on nothing less than a real-life specimen of a mermaid; a dangerous descendant of the human race was really and truly living in our oceans. Not only that, the NOAA supposedly had evidence that suggested the legendary Bloop recording of 1997 was somehow linked to the underwater activities of these gruesome fish-people, as well. Thus, another complex layer was added to the conspiracy. In order to ensure that public hysteria did not quickly break out across the entire planet, silence was the official order of the day.

Mermaids: The Body Found was nothing more than a practical joke, an April Fools' Day–style spoof—albeit a very good one, with a wealth of impressive special effects, stunning imagery, and a team of actors who, had the ruse not been revealed in the days that followed, really appeared to be NOAA-connected whistleblowers ready and willing to go public and expose the truth to an astounded world. Such was the anticipation provoked by the teasers for the show that appeared on the Animal Planet in the days and weeks leading up to the broadcast, it became the most watched show on the channel since its memorial production on the late Steve Irwin, the Crocodile Hunter, in 2006. But that was far from the end of the controversy.

No mermaids—honest!

Following the broadcast of the docudrama, the National Ocean Service (NOS), a branch of the National Oceanic and Atmospheric Administration, put out a forthright statement on its Website assuring the public that no evidence existed in support of the notion that mermaids were in any fashion real. The NOS's official statement read, in part, as follows:

> Mermaids—those half-human, half-fish sirens of the sea— are legendary sea creatures chronicled in maritime cultures since time immemorial. The ancient Greek epic poet Homer wrote of them in The Odyssey. In the ancient Far East, mermaids were the wives of powerful sea-dragons, and served as trusted messengers between their spouses and the emperors on land. The aboriginal people of Australia call mermaids yawkyawks—a name that may refer to their mesmerizing songs. But are mermaids real? No evidence of aquatic humanoids has ever been found. Why, then, do they occupy the collective unconscious of nearly all seafaring peoples? That's a question best left to historians, philosophers, and anthropologists ("No evidence of aquatic humanoids has ever been found," 2012).

And that's where the NOS chose to leave matters. Some who watched the Animal Planet's spoof wondered why both the NOAA and the NOS didn't loudly complain that they had been massively misrepresented, or assert that whole swathes of the population had been misled about the true nature of the work of the agencies. Others suggested that the NOS was not just protesting the truth about mermaids, but was actually protesting a bit *too* much. Certainly, the fact that the NOS even felt the need to create an entire new section on its Website—

an official Website of the U.S. government, no less—devoted to denying mermaids have any basis in reality was perceived in conspiracy circles as being way over the top and, perhaps, even a form of damage control.

Mermaids: The Body Found was, without a doubt, a hoax. And it was a brilliant hoax. But, did its fiction actually (and ironically) mirror deeply classified, top-secret fact? And if so, did this situation of "fiction meets fact" lead the NOAA and NOS to their very curious position of publicly and vociferously downplaying the entire matter of apes of the aquatic kind on a Website owned and maintained by the U.S. government? I'll leave that for you, dear reader, to decide.

CHAPTER 25

THE CAT IS OUT OF THE BAG

During the early part of 1998, the British government's House of Commons held a fascinating and arguably unique debate on the legendary Alien Big Cats, or ABCs, that were implicated in the very weird and conspiratorial affair of Jonathan Downes, the British Army, and Major James Hewitt and his famous secret lover, Diana, Princess of Wales. Documentation that was generated as a result of the February 2, 1998 debate on the controversy in the House of Commons began with a statement from Mr. Keith Simpson, the member of Parliament for mid-Norfolk. For more than two decades, he said, "there has been a steady increase in the number of sightings of big cats in many parts of the United Kingdom. These are often described as pumas, leopards or panthers. A survey carried out in 1996 claimed sightings of big cats in thirty-four English counties" ("Big Cats, Norfolk," 1998).

Many of the sightings, Simpson continued, had been reported in his constituency by people out walking their pet dogs or driving down old country roads, very often at the break of dawn or at dusk. Frequently the description given fitted perfectly with that of a puma or a leopard. Simpson also added that in a number of incidents, ewes, lambs, and even horses had been attacked and in some cases killed by the marauding beasts. Simpson elaborated that a number of distinguished wildlife experts had suggested to the government that some pumas or leopards could have been released into the countryside when the Dangerous Wild Animals Act of 1976 made it illegal to own such animals without a licence, which does, of course, tally very well with the previous claims of the late Louis Foley, who did exactly that in the 1970s. Simpson noted that the creatures would have been able to roam over a wide area of countryside, live off wild or domestic animals, and possibly even breed. So what, wondered Simpson, could be done about the problem?

THE PROBLEM OF BRITAIN'S BIG CATS

Answering his own question, Simpson said: "I should like to suggest two positive measures for the Minister to consider: at national and local levels, it is logical that the Ministry of Agriculture, Fisheries and Food should be the lead Government Department for coordinating the monitoring of evidence concerning big cats" (Ibid.). In response, Elliot Morley, who at the time was the Parliamentary Secretary to the Ministry of Agriculture, Fisheries and Food, admitted that there was indeed a valid issue that sorely needed to be addressed. He explained that the Ministry's main responsibility when it came to the matter of the nation's big cats was limited to one matter and one matter alone: namely, whether or not the animals posed a threat to livestock or possibly even to the human populace. As an aside, Morley added that the Ministry was aware that a total of 16 big cats had escaped into the wild since 1977: "They include lions, tigers, leopards, jaguars and pumas, but all but two animals were at large for only one day." And even those remaining two, he assured his colleagues, were very soon back where they belonged (Ibid.).

Due to the potential hazard that the ABCs posed, said Morley, the Ministry did indeed investigate each and every report brought to its attention in which it was claimed that livestock have been attacked and/or killed. He added: "Reports to the Ministry are usually made by the farmers whose animals have been attacked. In addition, the Ministry takes note of articles in the press describing big cat incidents and will consider them if there is evidence that livestock are at risk" (Ibid.). Upon receipt of a report of a big cat sighting, explained Morley, the Ministry would ask the Farming and Rural Conservation Agency (FRCA)—in essence, the Ministry's wildlife advisers—to contact the person who reported the encounter, at which point

> [t]he FRCA will discuss the situation with the farmer and seek to establish whether the sighting is genuine and whether any evidence can be evaluated. It will follow up all cases where there is evidence of a big cat that can be corroborated and all cases where it is alleged that livestock are being taken (Ibid.).

The FRCA, Morley added, would carefully consider all the available forms of data and evidence, which might include photographs provided by members of the British public and farmers, plaster casts of paw prints, and video footage. In addition, if circumstances allowed for it, field studies of the carcasses of farm animals that had allegedly fallen victim to ABC attacks would also be undertaken. Morley concluded by admitting that it was impossible to say with absolute certainty that Britain was *not* home to one or more populations of ABCs. For that reason alone, it was only right and proper that the Ministry should continue to investigate serious claims of their existence, but only when there was a perceived threat to life or livestock and/or when there was clear evidence that could be validated. Morley's last words of significance on the matter: "I am afraid that, until we obtain stronger evidence, the reports of big cats are still in the category of mythical creatures" (Ibid.).

Thanks to the Freedom of Information Act, we now have that clear evidence.

Armed police and cats at large

Replying in 2006 to a FOIA request from a member of the British public with an interest in big cat sightings seen in the English county of Hampshire between 1995 and 2005, the county's police force released secret files that stated the following:

> *Hampshire's Constabulary's Air Support Unit has been deployed to assist with the following reports: January 1995—Black Panther like animal seen in Eastleigh. Two likely heat sources found by the aircraft, but nothing found by ground troops. March 1995—Black Puma like animal seen in Winchester. One heat source found that could not be classified by the aircraft crew, kept running off from searching officers, search eventually abandoned* (Hampshire Police Report, 1995).

Notably, when a similar FOIA request was filed with Sussex police in late 2005, documentation was made available to

Something big, black, and beastly roams the U.K. © U.S. Fish and Wildlife Service, 2002. Source: Wikipedia

the requester that read as follows: "Firearms officers have been deployed in response to such a report on one occasion, on 22 July 2004—sighting by a member of the public in Seaford. The area was searched, but no trace was found of such an animal" ("Unidentified Cat," Sussex Police Report, 2004).

The story gets much more interesting on the east coast of England. In 1991, official police documents show that a fully grown lynx was shot dead near Great Witchingham, Norfolk. The shooter then placed the body in his freezer before selling it to a local collector, who decided to have the creature stuffed and mounted. The Department for Environment, Food and Rural Affairs subsequently came to the conclusion that it probably escaped from a nearby zoo, although this was never actually proven to be the case. An extensive, secret dossier on the affair was opened by local police that would have remained under lock and key just like the previous reports on other exotic felines prowling the British countryside, were it not for the very useful provisions of the government's Freedom of Information Act.

It all began when police officers were investigating a game-keeper who, it was suspected, may have been responsible for the deaths of a number of birds of prey that had been living in the area. The officer that interviewed the man in question wrote in his now-declassified official report:

> At the start of the search in an outhouse, which con-tained a large chest freezer, I asked him what he had in the freezer, and he replied: "Oh, only some pigeons and a lynx." On opening the freezer there was a large lynx lying stretched out in the freezer on top of a load of pigeons! He had shot this when he saw it chasing his gun dog (Barkham, 2006).

Britain's big cats, it seems, are no longer the myth that many wish or believe them to be—and the nation's government knows it, too.

IN SEARCH OF THE ESSEX LION

To demonstrate British officialdom's ongoing involve-ment in this issue, in August 2012, wild and sensational rum-ors spread around St. Osyth, Essex, that nothing less than a lion was on the loose. A 3-foot-long lynx, weighing in at around 30–40 pounds, and which would probably have done its very best to avoid people, was one thing, but a fully grown, man-eating lion—a beast that can reach lengths of in excess of 10 feet and weights of more than 500 pounds—was most certainly quite another. No wonder locals locked themselves behind closed doors for a few days!

British police immediately pulled out all the stops: 31 officers—some armed with high-powered rifles—were dispatched to seek out the creature, and the force's helicopter was commandeered to scour the fields and streets below. Ultimately, no lion was ever found, and the matter was relegated to the realm of misidentification; it had been a large pet cat and nothing else. This is very likely true, as no reports of any significance surfaced after August of 2012. Regardless of the false alarm, this affair still serves to demonstrate the seriousness with which the British government regards reports of big cats on the prowl. If the past is anything to go by, this will likely continue to hold true in the years to come.

Chapter 26

Werewolves and the Military

"Even a man who is pure of heart and says his prayers by night, may become a wolf when the wolf bane blooms and the autumn moon is bright," was the eerie message immortalized in the classic 1941 movie *The Wolf Man*. It's a message that many of the credulous have taken, and continue to take, very seriously. For those who firmly believe in the existence of werewolves, the stark image of a hairy, shape-shifting beast that is part human and part wolf, and that regularly embarks on killing sprees at the sight of a full moon, is most certainly no joke. If such creatures really do exist, are they true werewolves of the type that have been so successfully portrayed on the big screen by Hollywood movie moguls and special-effects experts? Could such "werewolves" possibly be deranged souls—lycanthropes in the thrall of deep delusion? Or might they even have distinctly paranormal origins? Paradoxically, the answer to all three of these controversial questions may very well be yes.

HALLUCINOGENIC HORRORS

Clinical lycanthropy is a rare psychiatric condition that is typified by an overwhelming delusion that the afflicted person has the ability to morph into the form of a wild animal—very often, that of a berserk, killer wolf of monstrous proportions. Interestingly, a 1999 paper titled *Lycanthropy: New Evidence of its Origin* written by H.F.Moselhy, demonstrated that two people diagnosed with clinical lycanthropy displayed evidence of unusual activity in the parts of the brain known to be involved in representing how we perceive body shape and image. In other words, clinical lycanthropes may very well believe that their bodies really are mutating when they are overwhelmed by their delusions—even if such changes are not noticeable to anyone else. Of course, this does not fully explain why sufferers believe they are changing into this one particular animal, a wolf, rather than just experiencing random changes in, say, their arms or legs. Nevertheless, the mysterious condition is undoubtedly a significant aspect of the overall werewolf controversy. And there is another aspect to this affair that may go some way toward explaining the inner workings of the mind of the clinical lycanthrope.

Linda Godfrey, a leading and recognized authority on werewolves, and the author of such books as *Real Wolfmen*, *Hunting the American Werewolf*, *The Beast of Bray Road*, and *Werewolves*, points to ergot, a fungus that affects rye, as a possible medical explanation for some claims of lycanthropy. According to this particular scenario, says Godfrey, it is not a demonic or otherwise paranormal influence that causes the alleged changes to the human body, but the ingestion of *Claviceps purpurea*, which contains a compound similar to LSD. As she notes, one of the chief side effects of ingestion of this fungus is that of terrifying delusions. Most interesting of all, for reasons that remain tantalizingly unknown, prevalent among such delusions is the sufferer's conviction that he or she is shape-shifting into the form of a wild, crazed beast.

SERIAL WOLFMEN

Beyond any shadow of doubt, one of the most notorious serial killers of all time was Peter Stumpp, a German farmer who became infamously known as the Werewolf of Bedburg. Born in the village of Epprath, Cologne, Stumpp was a wealthy, respected, and influential farmer in the local community. But he was also hiding a truly dark and diabolical secret, one that surfaced most graphically and sensationally in 1589, when he was brought to trial for the heinous crimes of both murder and cannibalism. Having been subjected to the extreme torture of the rack, Stumpp confessed to countless horrific acts, including feasting on the flesh of sheep, lambs, and goats, and even that of men, women, and children. Indeed, Stumpp further revealed that he had killed and devoured no fewer than 14 children, two pregnant women and their fetuses, and even his own son's brain. Stumpp, however, had an extraordinary excuse to try and explain and account for his vile actions.

Stumpp maintained that since the age of 12, he had secretly engaged in black magic, and on one occasion had succeeded in summoning up none other than the Devil, who provided him with a magical belt that gave Stumpp the ability to morph into the form of a huge wolf with large, glowing eyes, powerful limbs, and razor-sharp fangs. While the Devil may have been impressed or even amused by Stumpp's explanation for his animalistic activities, the court most assuredly was not. He was put to death in a most brutal fashion: Flesh was torn from his body, his arms and legs were broken, and, finally, he was beheaded. The Werewolf of Bedburg was no more. Stumpp was not the only such case, unfortunately.

Equally as horrific as the actions of Peter Stumpp were those of an unnamed Frenchman who, in the final years of the 16th century, became known as the Werewolf of Chalons. The Paris, France–based tailor killed, dismembered, and consumed the flesh of numerous children he had lured into his shop. The monster was brought to trial for his crimes on December 14, 1598. Notably, during the trial, it was claimed that on occasion the man also roamed nearby woods in the form of a huge, predatory wolf, where he further sought out innocent souls to slaughter and consume. As was the case with Stumpp, the Werewolf of Chalons was sentenced to death and duly burned at a stake. The idea that mental illness—possibly accompanied by the inadvertent ingestion of ergot—could account for some of the legends of werewolf activity is highly plausible and very likely in these two particular cases, as well.

What very few have recognized or probably have any awareness of is the fact that, for reasons that are as intriguing as they are difficult to explain, encounters with or sightings of werewolves seem to be most prevalent in the vicinity of military installations and their personnel. This has reportedly provoked official agencies of government to take far more than a passing interest in the subject of monsters of the full moon.

Werewolves and the military

In May 2007, I wrote an article for my blog titled "Do Were-wolves Roam the Woods of England?" My decision to write and publish the feature was prompted by the numerous sightings that year of a werewolf-type beast in the heart of the Cannock Chase, a large area of forest and heath in the English county of Staffordshire. Notably, all the encounters occurred within the confines of an old cemetery, specifically, a cemetery housing the remains of German soldiers and airmen who died in POW camps on British soil during the Second World War. It remains the most popular post at my blog and prompted one commenter, with the username of "Wes," to describe the following experience he had had concerning a werewolf and the military:

> I encountered a werewolf in England in 1970. I was twenty years old when I was stationed at RAF [Royal Air Force] Alconbury [in the county of Cambridgeshire]. I was in a secure weapons storage area when I encountered it. It seemed shocked and surprised to been caught off guard and I froze in total fright. I was armed with a .38 and never once considered using it. There was no aggression on its part. I could not comprehend what I was seeing. It is not human. It has a flat snout and large eyes. Its height is approximately five feet and [its] weight [is] approximately 200 pounds. It is very muscular and thin. It wore no clothing and was only moderately hairy. It ran away on its hind legs and scurried over a chain link fence and ran deep into the dense wooded area adjacent to the base. I was extremely frightened but the fear developed into a total commitment of trying to contact it again. I was obsessed with it. I was able to see it again a few weeks

later at a distance in the wooded area. I watched it for about thirty seconds slowly moving through the woods and I will never forget my good fortune to encounter it, and to know this "creature" truly does live among us (Redfern, 2007).

In January 2010, I spoke at a New York conference called Ghosts of Cooperstown, which was organized by the stars of

Werewolves: monsters of top-secret interest to the U.S. military. Unknown artist, 18th century. Source: Wikipedia

the SyFy Channel's *Ghost Hunters* series. It was on the Saturday night of the event that an American soldier, who had then recently returned from serving with the military in the Middle East, revealed to an audience in the hotel bar that he had heard tales of large, marauding werewolves roaming by night the mountains of Afghanistan and some of the more ancient parts of Iraq. The U.S. Army secretly knew that the beasts were out there, he said, but didn't know how to handle the situation. They lacked any real understanding of what the creatures were or where,

MONSTER FILES

exactly, they came from. And so the military chose to take the easiest of all approaches available to them: They simply ignored the reports or wrote them off as campfire tales.

I asked the man if there was any way I could get his data validated. He replied that there wasn't, unfortunately, but stressed that it was true all the same. His story might well have been the barest bones of what sounds like a much bigger, and far more significant saga, made all the more intriguing by the fact that deeply similar stories have reached the eyes and ears of the aforementioned Linda Godfrey.

THE WEREWOLF FILES

Raised in Milton, Wisconsin, Linda Godfrey is an author, journalist, and artist whose newspaper articles have garnered several awards, including a first-place feature story from the National Newspaper Association in 1995 and 1998. It was thanks her book *The Beast of Bray Road* and her time spent as Wisconsin's very own unofficial werewolf hunter that Godfrey is now leading the pack, so to speak, in the investigation of one of the strangest stories of modern times. Indeed, since the publication of *The Beast of Bray Road* in 2003, Godfrey has gone on to write several more books on the subject of real-life werewolves. It is to the beginning of Godfrey's work we need to turn, since it is directly relevant to the matter of werewolves and the world of officialdom. When I interviewed her in 2003, she had this fascinating story to recount:

> *The story first came to my attention in about 1991 from a woman who had heard that there were rumors going around here in Elkhorn, and particularly in the high school, that people had been seeing something like a*

werewolf, a wolf-like creature or a wolf-man. They didn't really know what it was. But some were saying it was a werewolf. And the werewolf tag [was] used because I think that people really didn't know what else to call it. And these days you have so much Hollywood influence that it colors your thinking about your observations. So when anybody sees something that's an out-of-place animal, you get those images. Well, I started checking it out. I talked about it with the editor at The Week newspaper here, and which I used to work for. He said: "Why don't you check around a little bit and see what you hear?" This was about the end of December. And being a weekly newspaper that I worked for, we weren't really hard news; we were much more feature oriented. So I asked a friend who had a daughter in high school and she said: "Oh yeah, that's what everybody's talking about." So, I started my investigations and got one name from the woman who told me about it, and she was also a part-time bus driver. She told me that she had called the county animal control officer. So, of course, when you're a reporter, anytime you have a chance to find anything official, that's where you go. I went out to see him and, sure enough, he had a folder in his file drawer that he had actually marked "Werewolf," in a tongue-in-cheek way. It wasn't by any means that he believed it was a werewolf; but people had been phoning in to him to say that they'd been seeing something. They didn't know what it was; but from their descriptions, that's what he had put. So, of course that made it a news story. When you have a public official, the county animal control officer, who has a folder marked Werewolf, that's news (Redfern, 2003).

Such a situation is indeed news. And this would not be the last time that Godfrey's path would cross with both werewolves and officialdom.

SHAPE-SHIFTERS, DIMENSION-HOPPERS, AND THE MILITARY

One of the most intriguing things that Linda Godfrey has learned in her more than 20 years of research into werewolf phenomena in the United States is that, just as appears to be the case in the U.K., Iraq, and Afghanistan, the beasts seem to be attracted to active military installations. One of these areas is the Fort Custer Recreation Area in Michigan; it amounts to around 3,000 acres of recreation land in that fell into the hands of the U.S. government back in 1917, and which, when known as Camp Custer, was used as a training center for Army inductees.

Late one night in 2000, the area had what was quite possibly its strangest visitor of all: a large, fox-like animal that had the ability to run on its hind legs. The fact that the creature was covered in hair, had a protruding muzzle, and, at times, moved like a human inevitably evoked imagery of the classic werewolf of legend and lore. But there's more: Just as the werewolf-infested cemetery on England's Cannock Chase was home to the remains of hundreds of German military personnel from the Second World War, so the old Michigan-based camp housed more than 500 Nazi troops in that same war-torn era, 26 of whom died on site and were subsequently buried there. Godfrey is well-acquainted with many other such stories: the story of a werewolf encounter in 1973 at an abandoned missile silo in Kansas; an August 1992 sighting of a large, hairy monster near Wisconsin's Fort Atkinson; a 1994 experience involving military personnel and a beast that resembled Anubis, the jackal-headed god of ancient Greece, at the Great Lakes naval base located near to the shore of Lake Michigan; and a 2004 report of a huge, wolf-like animal at Kansasville's Richard Bong State Recreation Park, which, interestingly, was previously Bong Air Force Base. But there is one case that stands out above all the rest and, just perhaps, gets to the heart of the relationship between werewolves and the American military.

In 2005, Linda Godfrey was contacted by a man trained in remote viewing—a subject that the U.S. government has researched for decades and which, as the testimony of Jim Marrs makes clear, was used in its quest to resolve the mystery of the Loch Ness Monster. It so happens that Godfrey's informant—who was himself employed as a consultant to the government—had attempted to remotely view these most mysterious of all canines. He came to the conclusion that they are a very ancient, extraterrestrial species that, notably, resembles the old Greek god of the underworld, Anubis. Godfrey's source also learned that the creatures "jump" from location to location via portals or gateways to what we might term other realms or dimensions. This may not be as far-fetched or outrageous as it sounds.

As was noted previously, the U.S. Air Force displayed keen interest in the matter of vanishing Bigfoot-style beasts in Pennsylvania back in the 1970s; more than 30 years later, it even commissioned a report on teleportation technology. There is a clear pattern developing here: Bigfoot, the Loch Ness Monster, werewolves: they have all attracted the secret attention of the United States military and government, and each and every one of these strange beasts appears to have the unnerving and uncanny ability to vanish into nothingness. Or, perhaps far more likely, they have exhibited evidence of crossing over from our world into other realms of existence, about which the U.S. military would dearly like to know a great deal.

CHAPTER 27

SOMETHING DWELLS DOWN UNDER

Just as the British government has publicly and vocally addressed the controversy surrounding the many reports of large, predominantly black cats of unknown type and origin roaming the United Kingdom, so the government of Australia has done the same. And just like their British cousins, the Aussies have been extremely reluctant to endorse the notion that such animals—Alien Big Cats, or ABCs—are prowling around their land, as official records now in the public domain demonstrate. Nevertheless, there's certainly no shortage of accounts suggesting the beasts are out there. Many have popped up in and around the Australian city of Sydney, the State Capital of New South Wales.

In September 2008, Nathan Rees, the Premier of New South Wales, Australia, made a very definitive public statement to the effect that he did not believe the big cats of Sydney could be written off as nothing stranger than a modern-day bit of folkloric entertainment. This was a far cry indeed from a statement that Rees had made only a few weeks previously—namely, that reports of big cats on the loose were merely the stuff of urban legend. Rees's rapid turnaround was hardly surprising, however: He confirmed that more than a stunning 600 reports, collected and collated at a local level, had just been brought to his personal attention.

Eyewitness encounters

As one recent and typical example of many, just such a creature was seen in May 2010 by Paul Cauchi and his girlfriend, Naomi, as they were driving through Yarrawonga, Australia. Cauchi said that although the black beast was only in view for a few seconds, both he and Naomi were absolutely certain that what they saw was not a large feral cat, but in fact a panther. Such was the large amount of publicity given to the report that even Steve Whan, the Minister for Primary Industries in New South Wales, admitted that other sightings of the creature had reached Sydney officialdom, adding somewhat reassuringly that government took all such reports very seriously. As for the question of where the cats may have come from, with any prosaic explanations sorely and mysteriously lacking, it has been suggested that they may represent the descendents of cougars brought to Australia as mascots by U.S. military forces during the Second World War, and then secretly released into the wild when the Americans headed off to do battle with the Japanese. True or not, it's a possibility to keep under consideration.

It is cases like that of Paul Cauchi and Naomi, as well as the dramatic reevaluation and u-turn of Premier Nathan Rees that led the Australian government to commission a study of the phenomenon. It was part of a concerted effort to determine the validity of the stories coming from the part of the country where a considerable number of reports of large cats on the loose had surfaced: the State of Victoria. The plan for the study was formally announced in 2010 by the Victorian National Party's Peter Ryan, who felt there were significant numbers of credible observations of anomalous big cats on record to warrant such an investigation. No doubt, the many farmers of the area who had reportedly lost considerable numbers of livestock to something large and deadly breathed a big, collective sigh of relief. Not for long, unfortunately.

THE BIG CAT REPORT

The title of the report was *Assessment of Evidence for the Presence in Victoria of a Wild Population of "Big Cats."* Prepared by Peter W. Menkhorst and Leigh Morison, it was published on September 18, 2012, amid a great deal of controversy, which is hardly surprising, given the nature of the mysterious issue under scrutiny. The controversy was also partly attributable to its conclusion, which was that a living population of big cats in Australia was considered to be extremely unlikely. The Honorable Peter Walsh, a member of Parliament and the Minister for Agriculture and Food Security, commented on the contents of the report. Noting the fact that, by his own admittance, there were now thousands of reports on file from this particular part of Australia alone, he assured the nation's media that no large cat had "ever been detected in a formal wildlife survey, shot by a hunter or farmer or killed by a vehicle and no skeletal remains have ever been found. Nor have 'big cats' been identified in wildlife studies involving the analysis of thousands of mammalian fecal samples" (Lannen, 2012).

So what, then, were people seeing, if not big cats almost identical to those encountered on the other side of the world in the British Isles? The many reports addressed by the study suggested they were something akin to pumas and cougars. The official stance, however, was that they were nothing stranger or more worrying than exceptionally large, domestic cats that had turned feral. This stance was somewhat in conflict with the fact that some of the preliminary DNA evidence actually pointed to the presence of big cats in Australia. Apparently the evidence, such as it was, could not be considered in any sense definitive. In other words, it appears that the government was equivocating: It was trying to lay the matter to rest as one of no major consequence while it tried to protect itself from criticism in the event that hard evidence did one day sensationally surface. When matters were finally wrapped up, the official stance was as follows: "On the basis of the report's conclusions, further work focusing on obtaining primary evidence to conclusively rule out the existence of 'big cats' is not warranted."

This was the final word of the Australian government, but it was hardly the last word on the matter, period. Certainly the biggest and most accurate criticism leveled at the report was that all of the research that led to its conclusions was done from within the sterile confines of government offices and research establishments. Indeed, this was the case: Not a single, in-depth field investigation was ever undertaken by those that had been commissioned to try and resolve the puzzle ("Big Cat Study Complete," 2012).

While studying the filed reports was, of course, an integral part of the project, surely actually visiting the locations where the cats were said to roam regularly would have been equally vital, if not even more so, for ensuring the completion of a balanced, unbiased study? Unfortunately, apparently not. This was *not* the fault of those tasked with carrying out the investigation; no, it was all blamed on the budget, or rather, the lack of budget, in this particular case. So, slender funds meant an inevitably slender study.

Andrew Nicholson, a researcher and writer who has studied both the Australian big cat saga and the Australian government's report itself, made a very good point in the wake of the publication of the government's findings on this very matter: "I wonder how many new species of plants and animals have been discovered from behind a desk?" (Nicholson, 2012) Not many, that's for sure! It must be stressed, however, that the senior zoologist who played a leading role in the project, Peter Menkhorst, did leave the door open to the possibility that big cats might be lurking in the wilds of Australia. As he said, "[T]he available evidence is inadequate to conclude a wild population does exist, but it does admit in some cases the identity of some animals is inconclusive. It's saying it's highly unlikely" ("Big Cats in Victoria," 2012).

The final word on all this properly goes to Andrew Nicholson: "[T]he Australian Big Cat Study that Wasn't leaves many unanswered questions as to the true nature of those large, black felines seen stealthily prowling the Victorian countryside" (Nicholson, 2012). Those big and mysterious cats of Australia were not the only unusual animals to have caught the attention of government bureaucrats, however.

A SURVIVOR AGAINST ALL ODDS

An undeniably weird-looking animal, the thylacine was a distinctively striped marsupial that resembled a strange combination of coyote, hyena, and tiger. As is typical of all marsupials, especially kangaroos, the creature, which grew to a length of around 6 feet, carried its young in a pouch. And it had the literally jaw-dropping ability to open its mouth to an angle of 120 degrees. As for its time spent on our planet, the thylacine is known to have lived for an incredibly long period in Australia, New Guinea, and Tasmania—hence its more popular name of the Tasmanian tiger. Fossilized examples of its distant ancestors date back to the Miocene period. In simple terms, we're talking about millions of years. Although examples of artwork displaying undeniable imagery of the thylacine can be found in aboriginal cave paintings that date back at least 3,000 years, the creature is thought to have been gone from the mainland long before the arrival of European settlers in the 1700s. Tasmania is a very different matter, however.

It was thanks to those surviving pockets of the creature on the island, which is located approximately 150 miles from the Australian mainland, that the thylacine lived on. Come the early years of the 20th century, however, deforestation led to the destruction of much of its natural environment, a large and fatal outbreak of disease followed, and the thylacine's time was finally up, aside from those few remaining examples that lived on until the mid-1930s in zoos and private enclosures. So much for the past. What about right now, in our time? Does the thylacine still roam, triumphantly defying the odds day by day and decade by decade?

The thylacine: perhaps not so extinct, after all. Unknown photographer, 1933.
Source: Wikipedia

Logic and common sense dictate that no one anywhere should be seeing a living thylacine now, in the 21st century. Not everybody is quite so sure the beast is truly gone for good, however. To its credit, even the Australian government keeps an open and balanced mind regarding the possibility that there may still be some around. While hard evidence of even one living thylacine is lacking, eyewitness testimony abounds, and much of it on file with the Australian government. The Tasmania Parks and Wildlife Service (TPWS) has been particularly open and forthcoming on this matter. Much of this is thanks to a man named Michael Moss, who, in the early 2000s, having an interest in ongoing sightings of the thylacine, used the Australian Freedom of Information Act to try to open the doors to whatever it was that the government knew about the animal. The good news is that Moss succeeded.

Of cases that post-date 1936, the year in which the last thy-lacine in captivity died in the confines of Tasmania's Hobart Zoo, the TPWS says:

> *Since 1936, no conclusive evidence of a thylacine has been found. However, the incidence of reported thylacine sight-ings has continued. Most sightings occur at night, in the north of the State, in or near areas where suitable habitat is still available. Although the species is now considered to be "probably extinct," these sightings provide some hope that the thylacine may still exist* (Tasmania Parks and Wildlife Service, 2013).

Prompted by many credible reports of thylacines seen in the vicinity of the Arthur River and the Pieman River of north-west Tasmania, an expedition was quickly and ambitiously launched in 1937 to try to find isolated pockets of the creatures, with no real success. Eight years later, notes the TPWS, an Aus-tralian naturalist named David Fleay spent time scouring the land along Tasmania's Jane River and found what very closely resembled thylacine paw prints. Similar prints were discov-ered in the northwest in 1959 by Eric Guiler, a man also fasci-nated by the possibility that the thylacine still existed. Then, in 1968, an extensive expedition was launched by the team of Bob Brown, James Malley, and Jeremy Griffiths, who uncovered a whole slew of recent eyewitness reports, but unfortunately no definitive smoking gun.

Even the TPWS's very own people were caught up in the controversy. In both 1982 and 1983, a TPWS employee, Nick Mooney, headed to Tasmania's Arthur River, where a wildlife officer named Hans Naarding claimed he had had his very own encounter with a living thylacine in 1982. Despite a detailed quest, Mooney failed to find any concrete evidence that the thylacine was not extinct. This had no effect on the frequency of reports, however. As the Freedom of Information Act has shown, more than a dozen reports—all strongly suggesting that there were thylacines about—were received by Tasmania's Parks and Wildlife Service between 1996 and the latter part of 2001.

This (so far) failure to come up with either a living or dead specimen in the modern era hasn't deterred those who still seek the thylacine. Certainly encouraging is officialdom's admittance that, even on the Australian mainland and moving away from Tasmania, sightings are hardly what one might term scarce. From 1936 to 1998, the Australian government's Department of Conservation and Land Management recorded 65 possible encounters from Western Australia alone, as available files now corroborate. Whether it's as dead as a dodo, clinging to life, or successfully thriving and hiding, the thylacine captivates not just those fascinated by the field of cryptozoology, but significant elements of Australian officialdom, too.

A TERRIFYING PREDATOR

Imagine coming face-to-face with a ferocious, carnivorous Monitor lizard with a length of somewhere between 15 and 20 feet—maybe even closer to 25 feet—and a weight in excess of at least a ton. Such a creature is widely assumed to have become extinct around 40,000 years ago. But what if that happened right now, deep in the heart of the subtropical rainforests of Australia? You think it couldn't happen? Many cryptozoologists say it has, and more than once. As for the creature in question, its name is *Megalania prisca*, a title bestowed on it by Richard

Owen, a 19th-century paleontologist who also famously came up with the term *Dinosauria*, or "terrible reptile." Its Latin taxonomic name translates roughly as "ancient giant butcher" or "ancient great roamer", which gives a pretty good indication of its less-than-hospitable nature. For years, reports have surfaced of creatures sounding suspiciously similar to this dangerous, enormous beast in the wilder parts of Australia; one of them is inextricably linked to officialdom. In August 1981, Australian cryptozoologist Rex Gilroy, who has doggedly pursued reports and claims of still-living *Megalania prisca* for decades, had the good fortune to meet with a soldier who may have come across evidence of the existence of just such a creature as recently as October 1968.

The Australian Army
ENCOUNTERS EVIDENCE

The witness, whose name was Steve, was part of a military unit engaged in an exercise on the Normandy Range, Queensland, designed to acclimatize the soldiers to jungle-based warfare. In a particularly swampy part of the region, Steve's team came across something most unexpected: the remains of a fully grown cow that appeared to have been violently torn apart by a powerful and very large predator. Further evidence of the sheer size of the creature was demonstrated by tracks on the ground that suggested the cow had been dragged a considerable distance before being partially devoured. Add to that an examination of roughly 20-inch-wide claw marks found in the mud, and what seemed to be the imprint of a powerful tail, and it all suggested the presence of a monster of somewhere in the region of an astonishing 30 feet in length. Whether it was *Megalania prisca* or something even bigger and far more ancient, Steve and his fellow soldiers didn't wait to find out: Not surprisingly, they got out of there as quickly as they could.

Maybe there's another answer to the riddle that has nothing to do with a real-life monster. Might this have been an ingenious, Australian equivalent of the U.S. military's early-1950s caper to bring to life in the jungles of the Philippines the legendary Aswang vampire, to spook enemy troops? Did someone at an official level in the Australian military ingeniously stage the event—using *Megalania prisca*, rather than a vampire, as their inspiration, to see how soldiers might respond on the battlefield when faced with something truly paradigm-busting and terrifying? That Steve's unit unanimously fled with hardly a glance behind them might have provided all the answers the higher echelons needed. Or, just maybe, *Megalania prisca* really does still hunt in Australia's ancient forests, and still pops up in the occasional army file now and again. Of course, either scenario would be undeniably amazing!

CONCLUSION

With all of these multifaceted and mysterious case files under our belts, it's time to try to make some degree of sense out of this bizarre and ever-growing menagerie filled to the brim with strange creatures and agents of government, the military, and the intelligence community, and which has existed for at least three centuries. If there is one thing we can say with certainty in this highly curious state of affairs, it is that the reasons for official interest in the bizarre beasts of cryptozoology are just about as varied and numerous as the creatures themselves. While some of the reasons for that interest are directly relative to the monsters in question, the nature of their existence, and their places of origin, others are clearly just about as far removed from such matters as is conceivably possible, and graphically demonstrate much weirder explanations for government interest in the realm of all things fierce, ferocious, and fantastically beasty.

Let us start with Bigfoot. One of the threads that run through several of the stories that appear in the pages of this book is that the infamous hairy beast of the woods is not the unknown ape that many cryptozoologists assume it to be, after all. If this is true, then the story of a Bigfoot having been secretly autopsied by elements of the U.S. military in 1962—a creature somehow intimately connected to UFO encounters at the Ohio-based John H. Glenn Research Center—is a perfect case in point, as are some of the tales of retrievals of Bigfoot corpses in relation to the Mount St. Helens disaster of 1980. Similarly, we can learn a great deal from the experiences of long-time UFO researcher and chaser of creatures, Stan Gordon of Pennsylvania, in the 1970s. Particularly in light of the 1962 saga at Ohio, it's most interesting that elements of officialdom should have taken so much interest in the Pennsylvanian wave, too, since that was also dominated by UFOs and anomalous lights seen in the same location, and at the same time, as Bigfoot.

That we do not appear to see any significant evidence of the U.S. government poking its collective nose into every tale of Bigfoot that surfaces under the sun, but specifically and only those instances where there is a thread comprised of UFOs and high strangeness, strongly suggests that someone, somewhere, in the heart of the official infrastructure secretly knows or suspects that Bigfoot is far more than many assume it to be. Ronan Coghlan's theory that Bigfoot may be a skilful negotiator of wormholes potentially offers us the biggest reason of all as to why certain parties in the U.S. government would be secretly studying the beast, its curious antics, and its link to UFOs: It is the technology or the psychic skills that the creature employs, rather than just its existence per se, that certain factions wish to understand and use for their own purposes, many almost certainly of a military nature.

When it comes to the Abominable Snowman of the Himalayas, it seems that while the creature itself might justifiably be said to be very similar to Bigfoot in nature and appearance, the reason for the Central Intelligence Agency's interest in it was far different from that shown in relation to the infamous, hairy man-beast of North America. The CIA astutely realized that by using certain individuals who demonstrated a genuine interest and flair in searching for the creature, but who also had solid links to the world of international espionage and skullduggery—the late Tom Slick being the perfect and prime example—they could undertake a whole variety of clandestine espionage operations on or near the Chinese border and, if confronted, could simply claim that nothing more suspicious than a Yeti hunt was afoot. Thus, for the spies of the CIA, the Abominable Snowman—even if it really did, and maybe still does, exist—was not so much a creature to be sought and caught as such, but one whose legendary status was to be used as a tool of Cold War–era deception and duplicity.

And what of the sea serpents? Well, the British Admiralty files of the 19th century certainly seem to demonstrate a significant degree of interest in those legendary, long-necked leviathans of the deep. And, that this same, decades-long interest appeared to extend to even carefully scrutinizing and cataloging newspaper reports as well as official accounts, suggests that someone in the Admiralty created their very own *X-Files*–style project on the subject. Perhaps an early and real-life equivalent of the fictional Fox Mulder? Despite all of this, there appears to be no evidence at all suggesting that the skeleton of such a gargantuan creature lies secretly buried deep in the British government's vaults, although such a scenario would be manifestly amazing if it were one day proved to be true! But, that someone, for reasons still unclear, was actively compiling dossiers on these mysterious animals for years, suggests that certain factions of the 19th-century naval forces of the United Kingdom knew enough about the beasts to keep them under careful and concerned watch.

Lake monsters are a very different kettle of fish. In terms of the Loch Ness Monster, it seems pretty safe to say that any official interest shown in the creature was for the most part routine. Regardless, it is still undeniably fascinating that the government was even interested to begin with! That the Joint Air Reconnaissance Intelligence Center (JARIC) played a significant, long-term role in analyzing film footage purporting to show the legendary creatures of the loch should not be interpreted as some kind of top-secret quest to try to ascertain the dark truth, and then summarily hide it from the public, the press, and the scientific community alike. Rather, it was simply that JARIC was happy to do a favor for a man who was passionate about the many mysteries of Nessie, and who had served his country both at the height of warfare and within government: David James, who, as we have seen, commanded a naval vessel during the Second World War and occupied a position in the British Parliament from 1959 to 1964,.

The lake-monster tales of Teggie of Lake Bala and Paddler of Lake Pend Oreille are another matter entirely. In those two instances, there seems to exist strong evidence that nether creature actually existed. The former was a fabrication of the British military, behind which was hidden an important pre–First World War secret concerning trained seals, explosives, and German targets. The latter was a U.S. Navy concoction designed to mask and confuse reports or leaks of secret submarine activity in the lake, particularly during the Second World War and the Cold War, when knowledge of advanced military submersibles had to be carefully hidden from any and all potential enemies of Uncle Sam. Spreading tales of the fearsome Paddler on the loose helped keep those same secrets very successfully buried. Much the same can be said about the flying Flatwoods Monster of West Virginia, and the monstrous Aswang bloodsucker of the Philippines. They, too, appear to have been the ingenious products of psychological warfare planners in the Pentagon who wished to see how monster legends could be secretly used for military capital and advantage. As the military was delighted to learn, those legends worked very well, indeed. Given the hysteria that was provoked at Flatwoods, maybe they worked just a bit *too* well.

In terms of the stories of Soviet ape-men of the 1920s and the CIA's Acoustic Kitty program four decades later, these were both perfect examples of what can happen—and what can go terribly and awfully wrong—when brilliant but crazed and eccentric scientists are given the freedom to do whatever they want when it comes to trying to turn regular, normal animals into ghoulish and freakish man-made monsters. Monsters and mad professors should always be kept well apart, lest disaster inevitably follow.

As for the so-called ABCs—the Alien Big Cats—of both Britain and Australia, a very good explanation can be offered as to why the governments of both lands would want to try to repeatedly downplay this particularly controversial matter—

namely, the fear of (1) public overreaction and panic in the event of official admittance that the phenomenon was a real one; and (2) tabloid media sensationalism that would surely only increase the public's anxiety even further. But in a truly unique, and certainly unforeseen, situation, it seems that the saga of Britain's big cats and the late Diana, Princess of Wales, became the subject of such in-depth, official, and top-secret controversy for a very different reason. If the details of the big cat encounter near the Devonshire home of Diana's lover, James Hewitt, reached the press, then those same details had the potential of opening up a massively sensational can of worms concerning Hewitt's affair with the woman who was the mother to the future heir of the British throne. History has shown, of course, how deeply the monarchy was indeed rocked when the truth of the Diana-Hewitt situation finally surfaced. Thus, anything that could potentially reveal the nature of their relationship had to be hidden at all costs—and that included burying the evidence of an Alien Big Cat seen roaming around in the vicinity of Hewitt's home. It also included keeping careful watch for years on Jonathan Downes, the director of the Center for Fortean Zoology and Hewitt's old school chum.

As for the very strange stories that combine werewolves, warfare, and military installations, which Linda Godfrey has so carefully collected and studied, here we find ourselves in largely uncharted waters, where far more questions than answers are forthcoming. However, given the fact that Godfrey has learned that these beasts may be dimension-hopping entities—not unlike Bigfoot, as sensationally hypothesized by Ronan Coghlan—might offer a very valid reason as to why military agencies, employing the use of remote viewers and psychic spies, might take a secret and concerted interest in them and their actions.

And then there are those fascinating cases where governments seem inexplicably open to the possibility that certain presumed-extinct creatures may still be alive, after all—the best example being the thylacine of Tasmania and Australia, which has been the subject of a great deal of government interest and the attendant official files. In this case we also have open admittance that the animal might still linger in certain wild places.

In sum, what we can say for sure with regard to the many and varied files, secrets, documents, and testimony at our disposal is that the bizarre issue of governments and monsters is not quite so simple as it seems. It is not merely a case of officialdom just going out searching for such things and then hiding the evidence as it (arrogantly) sees fit. No; instead, we're seeing a great deal of longstanding, classified interest in cryptozoology for many and varied reasons, some of which involve manufactured monsters, others that revolve around the exploitation of strange beasts for espionage purposes, and still others that appear to focus upon real, flesh-and-blood creatures of unknown provenance. Unknown to us, anyway, but perhaps not quite so unknown to the governments that are charged with guarding certain deep, underground vaults where—just perhaps—the wild things really do lurk.

BIBLIOGRAPHY

Note: Where authorship was identified, it has been included in the entries below. Certain Website links and documents, particularly those created by the government, tend to lack an author's name. In these cases, all data that is available has been provided.

ABC Statewide Drive. "Big Cats in Victoria: DSE study says they're just feral but case not closed." *www.abc.net.au/local /stories/2012/09/19/3593299.htm*. September 19, 2012.

"About Tom Slick." *www.mindscience.org/about/about-tom-slick*, 2013.

"Animals & Earthquake Prediction." *http://earthquake.usgs.gov/ learn/topics/animal_eqs.php*. August 9, 2012.

"Are We Ready for 'Bigfoot' or the Loch Ness Monster?" *http://permanent.access.gpo.gov/websites/fwsgov/news.fws.gov/historic/1977/19771221.pdf.* December 21, 1977.

"Bala Lake." *www.snowdoniaguide.com/lake_bala.html.* 2006.

Baring-Gould, Sabine. *The Book of Were-Wolves.* London: Smith, Elder and Co., 1865.

Barkham, Patrick. "Where the wild things are." *www.guardian.co.uk/uk/2006/mar/23/ruralaffairs.patrickbarkham.* March 22, 2006.

Bedard, Paul and Lauren Fox. "Documents Show Feds Believed in the Yeti." *www.usnews.com/news/blogs/washington-whispers/2011/09/02/documents-show-feds-believed-in-yeti.* September 2, 2011.

Benford, Gregory. *In the Ocean of Night.* New York: Warner Aspect, 2004.

"Big Cat." Hampshire, UK Police Report, August 12, 1995.

"Big Cat Study Complete." *www.premier.vic.gov.au/media-centre/media-releases/4891-big-cat-study-complete.html.* September 18, 2012.

"Big Cats, Norfolk." *Hansard*, February 2, 1998.

"Bloop." *http://oceanexplorer.noaa.gov/explorations/sound01/background/seasounds/seasounds.html#Anchor-1515.* July 16, 2012.

Borger, Julian. "Project: Acoustic Kitty." *www.guardian.co.uk/world/2001/sep/11/worlddispatch.* September 11, 2001.

Bowen, Scott. "Interview: Cryptozoologist Loren Coleman, Part 1." *http://trueslant.com/scottbowen/2010/05/27/interview-cryptozoologist-loren-coleman-part-1/.* May 27, 2010.

Brantley, Steve, and Bobbie Myers. "Mount St. Helens—From the 1980 Eruption to 2000." *http://pubs.usgs.gov/fs/2000/fs036-00/*. March 1, 2005.

Carey, Bjorn. "Gigantic Apes Coexisted with Early Humans, Study Finds." *www.livescience.com/467-gigantic-apes-coexisted-early-humans-study-finds.html*. November 7, 2005.

Clifton, Merritt. "Oliver, 55, chimp called the 'Humanzee.'" *www.animalpeoplenews.org/anp/2012/07/03/oliver-55-chimp-called-the-humanzee/*. July 3, 2012.

Cloud 9. "In Search of the Alma, wild snowmen of Russia." *http://open.salon.com/blog/cloud_9/2009/08/22/in_search_of_the_alma_wild_snowmen_of_russia*. August 22, 2009.

Coleman, Loren. *Bigfoot! The True Story of Apes in America.* New York: Paraview–Pocket Books, 2003.

——. "James Bond and Cryptozoology." *www.cryptozoonews.com/james-bond-cz/*. November 17, 2006.

——. "Mt. St. Helens Bigfoot Removal: National Guardsman Says It Is True." *www.cryptozoonews.com/mtstcoverup/*. September 17, 2012.

——. "Oil, Slick, Yeti, CIA...and Libya?" *www.cryptozoonews.com/slick-317/*. March 17, 2011.

——. "Tom Slick and JFK?" *http://copycateffect.blogspot.com/2012/03/tom-slick-jfk.html*. March 16, 2012.

——. *Tom Slick and the Search for the Yeti.* London: Faber & Faber, 1989.

——. *Tom Slick: True Life Encounters in Cryptozoology.* Fresno, Calif.: Linden Publishing, 2002.

——. "Tom Slick's Friend, Sir Victor Sassoon." *www.cryptozoonews.com/victor-sassoon/*. May 10, 2012.

Compton, James R. "Slick, Thomas Baker, Jr." *www.tshaonline.org/handbook/online/articles/fsl07*. 2013.

Conboy, Kenneth, and James Morrison. *The CIA's Secret War in Tibet*. Lawrence, Kans.: University Press of Kansas, 2002.

Couffer, Jack. *Bat Bomb: World War II's Other Secret Weapon*. Austin, Tex.: University of Texas Press, 2008.

Cryptoreporter. "Wales Lake Bala Monster Teggie." *http://cryptoreports.com/wales-lake-bala-monster-teggie*. April 3, 2012.

Currey, Cecil B. *Edward Lansdale: The Unquiet American*. Dulles, Va: Brassey's Inc., 1998.

Davidson, Keay. "Military examines 'beaming up' data, people/ Critics say its extreme computing, energy needs keep teleportation unlikely for now." *www.sfgate.com/science/article/Military-examines-beaming-up-data-people-2644406.php*. August 29, 2005.

Davis, Eric. "Teleportation Physics Study" *www.thelivingmoon.com/42stargate/03files/Wormhole_Technology.html*. 2006.

de Yampert, Rick. "Local UFO expert tracks Flatwoods Monster case." *www.news-journalonline.com/article/20121025/ENT/310249952*. October 25, 2012.

"Death Mills." *http://archive.org/details/DeathMills*. 2013.

Dinsdale, Tim. *The Leviathans*. Aylesbury, UK: Futura Publications, Ltd., 1976.

Douglass, James W. *JFK and the Unspeakable*. New York: Touchstone, 2010.

Downes, Jonathan. *CFZ Expedition Report: Guyana 2007*. Woolsery, UK: CFZ Press, 2008.

——. *Monster Hunter*. Woolsery, U.K.: CFZ Press, 2004.

"Dr. Michio Kaku." *www.mkaku.org*. 2013.

Drake, Frank, and Dava Sobel. *Is Anyone Out There?* New York: Delacorte Press, 1992.

Dunning, Brian. "Stalin's Human-Ape Hybrids." *http://skeptoid .com/episodes/4219*. August 17, 2010.

Edwardes, Charlotte. "CIA recruited cat to bug Russians." *www.telegraph.co.uk/news/worldnews/northamerica/ usa/1361462/CIA-recruited-cat-to-bug-Russians.html.* November 4, 2001.

"Ellingson Award." *www.asmaafg.org/html/ellingson_award .html.* 2013.

"Essex lion was my pet cat Teddy Bear—owner." *www.bbc.co.uk/ news/uk-england-essex-19397686.* August 28, 2012.

Faraci, Devin. "The Badass Hall of Fame: Tom Slick, Millionaire Yeti Hunter." *http://badassdigest.com/2011/09/06/the-badass-hall-of-fame-tom-slick-millionaire-yeti-hunter/.* September 6, 2011.

Feschino, Frank. *The Braxton County Monster.* Charleston, W. Va.: Quarrier Press, 2004.

Fisk, Ernest H., Counselor of Embassy, American Embassy, Kathmandu. *Regulations Governing Mountain Climbing Expeditions in Nepal—Relating To Yeti.* November 30, 1959. Available to view at the following link: *www .archives.gov/global-pages/larger-image.html?i=/historical -docs/doc-content/images/yeti-expedition-nepal-foreign-service-memo-l.jpg&c=/historical-docs/doc-content/ images/yeti-expedition-nepal-foreign-service-memo .caption.html.*

Gerhard, Ken and Nick Redfern. *Monsters of Texas.* Woolsery, UK: CFZ Press, 2010.

"Giant Reptilian Monsters in the Australian Bush." *www .mysteriousaustralia.com/australian_giant_reptilian_ monsters-qld.html.* 2013.

Global Research. "How CIA helped Dalai Lama to end up in exile." *www.globalresearch.ca/how-cia-helped-dalai-lama-to-end-up-in-exile/12804*. March 18, 2009.

Good, Timothy. *Alien Liaison: The Ultimate Secret*. London: Arrow Books, Ltd., 1991.

Godfrey, Linda. *Hunting the American Werewolf*. Madison, Wisc.: Trails Books, 2006.

——. *Real Wolfmen*. New York: Tarcher, 2012.

——. *The Beast of Bray Road*. Madison, Wisc.: Prairie Oak Press, 2003.

Gordon, Stan. *Silent Invasion: The Pennsylvania UFO-Bigfoot Casebook*. Greensburg, Pa.: Stan Gordon Productions, 2010.

Great Sea Serpent Again, The. Unidentified newspaper clipping, 1863, contained in British Admiralty file, reference number BJ 7/49.

"Gregory Benford." *www.gregorybenford.com/*. 2013.

Griffin, Buddy. "The Legend of the Flatwoods Monster." *www.wvculture.org/goldenseal/Fall02/legend.html*. 2012.

Hacker, Simon. "Days Out: The shy monster of Bala lake." *www.independent.co.uk/travel/news-and-advice/days-out-the-shy-monster-of-bala-lake-662073.html*. February 24, 2002.

Haile, Bartee. "Texan hunts abominable snowman." *http://haysfreepress.com/2010/12/08/texan-hunts-abominable-snowman/#axzz2MgCOlvoT*. December 8, 2010.

Hanks, Micah. "Bigfoot and Big Brother: The Weird Exploits of the Crypto-Feds." *http://mysteriousuniverse.org/2011/01/bigfoot-and-big-brother-the-weird-exploits-of-the-crypto-feds/*. January 15, 2011.

Hansen, Frank. "I Killed the Ape-Man Creature of Whiteface." *Saga*, July 1970.

Hardy, Alister. "Was Man More Aquatic in the Past?" *New Scientist*, March 17, 1960.

Harrington, Commander George Henry. Report to the British Admiralty, file reference number, MT/9/207, December 13, 1857.

Holiday, F.W. "Exorcism and UFO Landing at Loch Ness." *Flying Saucer Review*, Vol. 19, No. 5, September/October 1973.

——. *The Great Orm of Loch Ness*. London: Faber & Faber, Ltd., 1968.

Horne, Marc. "Yes Minister, we'll save Nessie from the poachers." *Sunday Times*, January 8, 2006.

Hungerford, Jean M. *The Exploitation of Superstitions for Purposes of Psychological Warfare*. RAND, April 14, 1950.

Huyghe, Patrick. "A Supernatural Cover-Story: Did the U.S. Navy tell Idaho residents a whopper of a fish story?" *www.astralgia.com/webportfolio/omnimoment/archives/features/supernatural/2.html*. 1997.

"Icequakes (Bloop)." *www.pmel.noaa.gov/vents/acoustics/sounds/bloop.html*. 2013.

James, William. "Extrasensory Perception (ESP)." *www.william-james.com/Science/ESP.htm*. 2013.

"John Chambers CIA 'identity transformation' field kit." *http://bid.profilesinhistory.com/John-Chambers-CIA-identity-transformation-field-kit_i11537211*. 2013.

Johnson, Eric Michael. "Scientific Ethics and Stalin's Ape-Man Superwarriors." *http://blogs.scientificamerican.com/primate-diaries/2011/11/10/stalins-ape-man-superwarriors/*. November 10, 2011.

Johnson, R.T. "John Chambers—The Real Master of Disguise: Studio 6, Argo, and the Iranian Hostage Crisis." *http://historyrat.wordpress.com/2012/11/04/john-chambers-studio-6/*. November 4, 2012.

Joint Air Reconnaissance Intelligence Center. "Photographic Interpretation Report Number 66/1." 1965.

"Joseph Banks Rhine." *www.nndb.com/people/029/000049879/*. 2012.

Krantz, Dr. Grover S. *Bigfoot Sasquatch Evidence*. Surrey, British Columbia: Hancock House, 1999.

——. *The Process of Evolution*. Rochester, Vt.: Schenkman Books, 1984.

Krystek, Lee. "Gigantopithecus." *www.unmuseum.org/bigape.htm*. 1996.

"Lake Pend Oreille: Idaho's superlative lake." *www.sandpointonline.com/rec/lakeguide/index.html*. 2013.

Lannen, Danny. "Hunt goes on for big cat." *www.geelongadvertiser.com.au/article/2012/09/19/351201_news.html*. September 19, 2012.

Lansdale, Edward Geary. *In the Midst of Wars*. New York: Fordham University Press, 1991.

LaPonsie, Daniel. "Yeti-Slick Document Causes Stir, Tom Slick's Life Story Gets Much Deserved Attention." *www.datelinezero.com/2011/09/19/yeti-slick-document-causes-stir-tom-slicks-life-story-gets-much-deserved-attention/*. September 19, 2011.

Lapseritis, Jack. *The Psychic Sasquatch*. Columbus, N.C.: Wild Flower Press, 2005.

Madrigal, Alexis, C. "Old, Weird Tech: The Bat Bombs of World War II." *www.theatlantic.com/technology/archive/2011/04/old-weird-tech-the-bat-bombs-of-world-war-ii/237267/*. April 14, 2011.

Maire III, Louis F., and J.D. LaMothe. *Soviet and Czechoslovakian Parapsychological Research*. Washington, D.C.: Defense Intelligence Agency, 1975.

"Major General Theodore Cleveland Bedwell, Jr." *www.af.mil/ information/bios/bio.asp?bioID=4642*. 2013.

Mality, Dr. Abner. "The Wild Men of Russia." *www.floridaskunkape .com/2010/03/28/the-wildmen-of-russia/*. March 28, 2010.

Marcum, Thomas. "President Theodore Roosevelt's Bigfoot Tale." *http://www.thecryptocrew.com/2012/01/president-theodore-roosevelts-bigfoot.html*. January 28, 2012.

Marrs, Jim. *Psi Spies*. Franklin Lakes, N.J.: New Page Books, 2007.

Marsh, Roger. "Bigfoot-UFO researcher George Lutz gets candid—an 8-part video interview." *www.examiner.com/article/ bigfoot-ufo-researcher-george-lutz-gets-candid-an-8-part-video-interview*. January 8, 2009.

Maskelyne, Jasper. *Magic: Top Secret*. London: S. Paul Publishers, 1949.

"Megalania, giant ripper lizard." *www.bbc.co.uk/nature/wild-facts/factfiles/3046.shtml*. 2013.

"Mermaids: The Body Found." *http://animal.discovery.com/tv-shows/mermaids/videos/mermaids.htm*. 2013.

MI5. *The Use of Pigeons in This War*. File reference number, HS 8/854, 1945.

"More than 100 pumas and leopards may be at large in Britain." *Yorkshire Post*, January 29, 2000.

Moselhy, H.F. "Lycanthropy: New Evidence of its Origin." *www .biomedsearch.com/nih/Lycanthropy-new-evidence-its-origin/10364725.html*. 1999.

Nashel, Jonathan. *Edward Lansdale's Cold War*. Amherst, Mass.: University of Massachusetts Press, 2005.

"National Oceanic and Atmospheric Administration." *www.noaa*
.gov/. 2013.

"Naval Acoustic Research Center." *www.cityprofile.com/idaho/*
naval-acoustic-research-center.html. 2012.

Nicholson, Andrew. "The Australian Big Cat Study That Wasn't."
http://mysteriousuniverse.org/2012/09/the-australian-big-
cat-study-that-wasnt/. September 21, 2012.

Nixon Cooke, Catherine. *Tom Slick, Mystery Hunter*. New York:
Paraview, 2005.

"No evidence of aquatic humanoids has ever been found." *http://*
oceanservice.noaa.gov/facts/mermaids.html. June 26, 2012.

Norwegian National Committee for the Evaluation of Research
on Human Remains. "Statement concerning the remains
of Julia Pastrana." *www.etikkom.no/no/Vart-arbeid/Hva-*
gjor-vi/Uttalelser/Skjelettutvalget/Statement-concerning-
the-remains-of-Julia-Pastrana/. June 4, 2012.

"On the hunt for the big cat that refuses to die." *www.cfzaustralia*
.com/2010/06/on-hunt-for-big-cat-that-refuses-to-die
.html. June 20, 2010.

Pain, Stephanie. "Blasts from the past: The Soviet ape-man
scandal." *www.newscientist.com/article/mg19926701.000-*
blasts-from-the-past-the-soviet-apeman-scandal.html.
August 23, 2008.

Pednaud, J. Tithonus. "Oliver—The Humanzee. *http://*
thehumanmarvels.com/72/oliver-the-humanzee/other.
2008.

"Peter Stumpp, Werewolf of Bedburg." *www.werewolves.com/*
peter-stumpp-werewolf-of-bedburg/. July 3, 2010.

Phillips, David Atlee. *The Night Watch: 25 Years of Very Peculiar*
Service. New York: Atheneum, 1977.

"Premier sinks claws into big cat mystery." *www.cfzaustralia* *.com/2008/09/premier-sinks-claws-into-big-cat.html*. September 20, 2008.

"Private Life of Sherlock Holmes, The." *www.imdb.com/title/* *tt0066249/*. 2013.

Randle, Kevin. "The Flatwoods Monster." *http://kevinrandle.* *blogspot.com/2011/03/flatwoods-monster.html*. March 23, 2011.

Ranelagh, John. *The Agency: The Rise and Decline of the CIA.* New York: Simon & Schuster, 1986.

Rappaneau, Dale. "Peter Stumpp: The Werewolf of Bedburg." *www.frightcatalog.com/blog/2011/06/24/peter-stumpp-* *the-werewolf-of-bedburg/*. June 24, 2011.

Redfern, Nick. "Do Werewolves Roam the Woods of England?" *http://monsterusa.blogspot.com/2007/05/do-werewolves-* *roam-woods-of-england.html*. May 17, 2007.

——. Interview with Jonathan Downes, May 14, 2006.

——. Interview with Joshua P. Warren, July 7, 2010.

——. Interview with Linda Godfrey, February 3, 2003.

——. *NASA Autopsies a Bigfoot.* Self published pamphlet, 2011.

———. *The World's Weirdest Places.* Pompton Plains, N.J.: New Page Books, 2012.

——. *Wildman! The Monstrous and Mysterious Saga of the "British Bigfoot."* Woolsery, UK: CFZ Press, 2012.

Report on the Select Committee on Assassinations of the U.S. House of Representatives. Washington, D.C.: U.S. Government Printing Office, 1979.

Rhine, Dr. Joseph Banks. *Final Report for Contract.* August 28, 1953.

Roberts, John and Elizabeth A. Roberts. *Freeing Tibet: 50 Years of Struggle, Resilience, and Hope.* New York: Amacom Books, 2009.

Roosevelt, Theodore. *The Wilderness Hunter.* New York: G.B. Putnam's Sons, 1906.

Rowland, Teisha. "Abominable Snowman! Footprints in the Snow." *www.independent.com/news/2010/dec/28/abominable-snowman/?print.* December 28, 2010.

Sanderson, Ivan T. *Abominable Snowmen: Legend Come to Life.* Kempton, Ill.: Adventures Unlimited Press, 2006.

——. "The Missing Link." *Argosy,* May 1969.

Sasser, Damon C. "Tom Slick and the Hand of the Yeti." *http://rehtwogunraconteur.com/?p=8613.* February 28, 2011.

Scottish Tourist Board, "Loch Ness Center and Exhibition," *www.lochness.com/.* 2006.

"Sea Serpent" Sighting. 315th Air Command Group, September 19, 1965.

Shawn. "Anonymous Former National Guardsman Claims Mt. St. Helens Burnt Bigfoot Story Happened." *http://bigfootevidence.blogspot.com/2012/09/anonymous-former-national-guardsman.html.* September 15, 2012.

Short, Bobby. "The Bigfoot Classics: The Bauman Story." *www.bigfootencounters.com/classics/bauman.htm.* 1995.

SilentReed. "The Aswang Vampire in Philippine Folklore." *http://silentreed.hubpages.com/hub/aswang.* April 11, 2012.

Simmonds, Ian. "The Abominable Snowman." *Fortean Times,* No. 83, October 1995.

"Soviet Sees Espionage in U. S. Snowman Hunt." *New York Times,* April 27, 1957.

Starkey, Jerome. "Stalin's mutant ape army." *www.thesun.co.uk/ sol/homepage/news/193024/.html*. August 3, 2007.

Stockdale, Captain James. Report to the British Admiralty, file reference number, BJ 7/49, May 9, 1930.

Strickler, Lon. "Bigfoot Recovery: Mt. St. Helens/Battle Mountain Complex." *http://naturalplane.blogspot.com/2012/09/ bigfoot-recovery-mt-st-helens-eruption.html*. September 17, 2012.

——. "Legendary Humanoids: Aswang, Shapeshifting Vampire." *http://naturalplane.blogspot.com/2010/09/legendary-humanoids-aswang.html*. September 2, 2010.

——. "The Mt. St. Helens Bigfoot Body Claims." *http://naturalplane .blogspot.com/2011/07/mt-st-helens-bigfoot-body-claims .html*. July 14, 2011.

Stringfield, Leonard. *Situation Red: The UFO Siege*. London: Sphere Books Ltd., 1977.

Stromberg, Joseph. "B.F. Skinner's Pigeon-Guided Rocket." *http://blogs.smithsonianmag.com/aroundthemall/2011/08/ b-f-skinners-pigeon-guided-rocket/*. August 18, 2011.

"Sound Surveillance System (SOSUS)." *www.pmel.noaa.gov/ vents/acoustics/sosus.html*. 2013.

Telepathy in Animals. Defense Intelligence Agency, October 1975.

"Unreal Worlds—Top Secret Snowmen." *www.theilluminerdy .com/2011/12/02/unreal-worlds-top-secret-snowmen/*. December 2, 2011.

"Three Sisters, Deschutes County, Oregon April 2007." *www .bigfootencounters.com/stories/deschutescntyOR.htm*. 2013.

"Thylacine." *www.parks.tas.gov.au/index.aspx?base=971*. 2013.

"Thylacine, or Tasmanian Tiger, Thylacinus cynocephalus." *www.parks.tas.gov.au/index.aspx?base=4765*. 2013.

"Thylacine, The." *http://australianmuseum.net.au/The-Thylacine*. November 22, 2012.

Tims. F.M. "New Indicators of Psychological Operations Effects." *http://www.dtic.mil/cgi-bin/GetTRDoc?AD=ADA015004*. 1975.

Town Cryer. "B.F. Skinner and the Pigeon-Guided Missile." *www.humortimes.com/2701/b-f-skinner-the-pigeon-guided-missile/*. August 18, 2011.

"Trips: Brooks Air Force Base, Texas, 21 November 1963." *www.jfklibrary.org/Asset-Viewer/Archives/JFKPOF-109-011.aspx*. 2013.

"Tuning in to a Deep Sea Monster." *http://articles.cnn.com/2002-06-13/tech/bloop_1_giant-squid-sound-surveillance-system-whales?_s=PM:TECH*. June 13, 2002.

U.S. Army. *Vietnam: PSYOP Directive: The Use of Superstitions in Psychological Operations in Vietnam*. May 10, 1967.

"Unearthly Batman Terrifies Watchers." *Houston Chronicle*, June 20, 1953.

"Unidentified Cat." Sussex Police Report, 2004

"Unit History: Joint Air Intelligence Reconnaissance Center." *www.forces-war-records.co.uk/Unit-Info/3536*. 2013.

Unknown Explorers. "Yeti." *www.unknownexplorers.com/yeti.php*. 2006.

"Varanus (Megalania) priscus." *http://museumvictoria.com.au/melbournemuseum/discoverycentre/dinosaur-walk/meet-the-skeletons/megalania/*. 2013.

Views on Trained Cats. Central Intelligence Agency. March, 1967.

Warren, Joshua P. *Pet Ghosts: Animal Encounters From Beyond the Grave.* Franklin Lakes, N.J.: New Page Books, 2006.

Waterhouse, David. *The Origins of Himalayan Studies.* London: Routledge, 2005.

Westenhöfer, Max. *Der Eigenweg des Menschen.* Berlin: Mannstaedt & Co., 1942.

Witchell, Nicholas. *The Loch Ness Story.* London: Corgi Books, 1982.

"Wolf Man, The." *http://www.imdb.com/title/tt0034398/.* 2013.

Wolman, David. "Calls from the Deep." *www.science.org.au/nova/newscientist/102ns_001.htm.* June 15, 2002.

Worley, Don. "The Winged Lady in Black." *Flying Saucer Review, Case Histories.* No. 10, June 1972.

Zona, Kathleen. "Glenn Research Center." *www.nasa.gov/centers/glenn/home/index.html.* 2013.

INDEX

MONSTER FILES

ACKNOWLEDGMENTS

I would like to offer my very sincere thanks and deep appreciation to everyone at New Page Books and Career Press, particularly Michael Pye, Laurie Kelly-Pye, Kirsten Dalley, Kara Kumpel, Gina Talucci, Jeff Piasky, and Adam Schwartz; and to all the staff at Warwick Associates for their fine promotion and publicity campaigns. I would also like to say a very big thank you to my literary agent, Lisa Hagan, for all her hard work and help.

About the Author

Nick Redfern works full-time as an author, lecturer, and journalist. He writes about a wide range of unsolved mysteries, including Bigfoot, UFOs, the Loch Ness Monster, alien encounters, and government conspiracies. His previous books include *The World's Weirdest Places*; *The Pyramids and the Pentagon*; *Keep Out!*; *The Real Men in Black*; *The NASA Conspiracies*; *Contactees*; and *Memoirs of a Monster Hunter*. He writes for many publications, including *UFO Magazine*, *Fate*, and *Fortean Times*. Nick has appeared on numerous television shows, including Fox News; The History Channel's *Ancient Aliens*, *Monster Quest*, and *UFO Hunters*; VH1's *Legend Hunters*; National Geographic Channel's *The Truth about UFOs* and *Paranatural*; BBC's *Out of this World*; MSNBC's *Countdown*; and SyFy Channel's *Proof Positive*. He can be contacted at *nickredfernfortean .blogspot.com*.